LIFE EXAMINED

LIFE EXAMINED

Why I Am a Christian

TIMOTHY J. MURRAY

RESOURCE *Publications* · Eugene, Oregon

LIFE EXAMINED
Why I Am a Christian

Resource Publications
An Imprint of Wipf and Stock Publishers
199 W. 8th Ave., Suite 3
Eugene, OR 97401

www.wipfandstock.com

PAPERBACK ISBN: 978-1-6667-1101-1
HARDCOVER ISBN: 978-1-6667-1102-8
EBOOK ISBN: 978-1-6667-1103-5

FEBRUARY 2, 2022 3:15 PM

CONTENTS

SECTION 1.1
EXAMINING LIFE: OUR KNOWLEDGE OF THE WORLD

SECTION 1.2
EXAMINING LIFE: OUR KNOWLEDGE OF OURSELVES

SECTION 3.2

EXAMINING EXPERIENCE: CHANGE

SECTION 3.3

EXAMINING EXPERIENCE: DESIRE

SECTION 4.1

EXAMINING THE OPTIONS: WHY CHRISTIANITY?

PREFACE

This book is written for those who are willing to think about how to make sense of life. Socrates is reported to have said that "the unexamined life is not worth living," but so often we are too busy getting on with all the demands and experiences of life to really think about what we are doing and how to make sense of it. Life is relentless. It takes over: work, play, relationships, family, friends, eat, drink, chores, sleep . . . And yet many of us live with a gut feeling that something is not quite right, that somewhere we're missing something. We wonder (or we would, if we ever had time) whether we're really on the right track or not . . .

But life is worth examining. Many people get to the end of it and wonder what happened. We can go through life accidently, rather than living on purpose. We can end up thinking, one day, "How on earth did I get here?" It is possible to be so caught up in life that we miss what living is all about. Jesus is reported to have said both that "the truth will set you free" and that he had come "to bring life to the full." He claimed that his worldview is the one that is best able to make sense of life, and his way of living enables us to experience life in the best possible way. I am a Christian because I believe that Jesus was right; this book attempts to explain some of the reasons I have come to that conclusion.

I have written primarily for those who are exploring the big questions of life for the first time, who are relatively unfamiliar with the Christian worldview and who are not necessarily big readers. To try to make this book as helpful as possible, each chapter is short (no more than five pages) and tries to tackle one main idea. In this sense, each chapter stands alone and can be taken separately, but in another sense it is the different chapters taken together that present a cumulative case for why Christians consider their worldview to be rationally robust and the most convincing way to make sense of life. I have covered several different kinds of ideas; some are more philosophical, for example, whereas others primarily address our experiences. If you find a particular chapter unclear or simply unhelpful, please feel free to move on to other chapters that may be more resonant. I hope that those which are helpful encourage you to explore more deeply. If you wish to do so and find my treatment too brief, I encourage you to pick up a couple of other books from the appendix at the back that tackle the ideas presented in this book at greater length.

Finally, I am aware that there will be others who pick up this book who have read more widely. It is worth saying at the outset that because of the purpose of this book, I have chosen to focus narrowly on the main idea of each chapter. There are fine distinctions that must be made, which I have not made; there are nuances that should be developed, which I have not developed. This is not because I am unaware of the complexities, but because this is not the book to engage with them. Again, I refer you to the appendix. I must say, though, that I do consider every main idea I present to be coherent, robust, and ultimately defensible.

ACKNOWLEDGMENTS

This project was first conceived whilst I was running a series of pub-based events with Chris Smith, to whom I am grateful for being willing to have a go at something a bit different and for knocking around some of the ideas that have eventually been incorporated into this book. The bulk of the work was completed as part of my role serving as one of the pastors of Amblecote Christian Centre. I am grateful to the elders and the wider church family for not only allowing me the freedom to study and write but also for your active encouragement to do so. My main aspiration for this book is that it will serve our church family well. Thanks are also due to several others: John Nelson was willing to critique several chapters; Bruce Murray and Beckie Welch sacrificed their time to proofread the entire manuscript; David Faulkner invested financially in the project. I appreciate your support in these varied ways. Finally, I want to acknowledge the contribution of my wife Jo. It is most easily seen in her constant encouragement of my labors but most deeply important in her willingness to lean together into the life to which God has called us.

Soli Deo Gloria

INTRODUCTION

Reasonable Faith

Many people distinguish between those who "have a faith" and those who do not, with Christians falling into the former category. I have had conversations with those who would describe themselves as atheist or agnostic, who suggest that whereas I (and others) live on the basis of faith, they are reliant on logic, rationality, and science. In other words, they distinguish between faith and reason, assigning themselves to the latter and religious believers to the former. I consider that distinction to be unreasonable, illogical, and irrational; with a little reflection, we can see that all of us live with both reason and faith. Before going any further, though, I should offer some simple definitions of how I am using these terms.

Definitions

By *reason*, I refer to our capacity to think rationally, by which I mean the ability to weigh and consider multiple possibilities and logically distinguish between what is probable and improbable, possible and impossible; to set out the grounds for our opinions and statements and to be able to discuss their validity; to seek explanatory principles and causes for phenomena we observe and the ability to justify and defend our assertions. By *faith* (or *belief*), I refer to the opinions that we hold about anything that cannot be proved absolutely. Religious faith, or religious belief, is merely that which involves a concept of a divine being; there are many other beliefs that are not directly connected to religion at all, but they are still a matter of faith. When we define our terms like this, we can see that there is no necessary conflict between faith and reason. Perhaps some examples will help.

Everybody has faith

We all hold many beliefs that we cannot prove to be correct; we all have faith. I wonder if you have seen the film *The Matrix*. The main concept of the narrative is that the world we think we live in is really a computer program into which we are plugged, whilst, unaware, our real bodies are being harvested by machines as an energy source. Now, can you prove to me that we are not living in the matrix? Can you even prove it to yourself? To take another vivid example, a person may suggest that the world came into existence a hundred years ago, and it started with all the signs of being old (some people began existing in old age with memories, the world began with fossils, old documents, etc). Can you prove that this isn't the case? I doubt it, but I also doubt you believe either of these suggestions.

To get to ideas that are more important and more personal, let us think for a moment about happiness. For millennia, philosophers have recognized that humans tend to act in accordance with what they believe will make them happy; but how does one prove what this is? What seems to make us happy this evening may devastate us in the long run. This may be obvious in the case of the alcoholic, but none of us can prove that what we *believe* is good for us now will result in our happiness down the road. How can I be 100 percent sure that this decision, rather than that one, will deliver the happiness I desire?

One last example: science itself. Science is based on observing or recording empirical evidence and interpreting the data with hypothesis, deduction, and evaluation. But how do I know that my senses (which I use to observe scientific data) are reliable? If I were to seek proof that they are, I would have to do so by using the very senses I need to test. We can test the reliability of our brain only by using it, but in doing so we must exercise faith that it is reliable. We assume its reliability. When we really think about it, those who assert that they "only believe what can be proven scientifically" are making a statement of belief that cannot be scientifically proven. The truth, then, is that everybody has a faith, because we all believe things that we cannot prove.

Everybody uses reason

Having said this, I don't imagine that any of those reading this book believe we live in the matrix or that the world is one hundred years old. We cannot prove ourselves correct in any absolute sense, but we hold it to be the most *reasonable* thing to think. This is the other side of the coin: none of us lives without reason. We all must choose what we believe. None of us believes everything, for the simple reason that many things are mutually exclusive: I cannot believe that the earth is round and flat at the same time. Therefore, we are always making decisions about what to believe is true, and we all use our reason to do this. I cannot prove to you that Wayne Rooney is not secretly the president of the USA, but it is much more likely that this is not the case. We do this all the time. I know of nobody who consciously thinks something is true that the person also considers irrational. It seems to me that everything in life that we think of as true is, more accurately, what we consider *the most reasonable belief to hold about something.*

A reasonable faith

So how, then, do we decide what is most reasonable to believe? *First*, we choose beliefs that have inner consistency; they can be held together logically, without contradiction. Again, we do this all the time. If I believed sweets were healthy but processed sugar was unhealthy, you would point out that my current beliefs were untenable because they were inconsistent. *Second*, we choose beliefs that cohere with our knowledge and experience of life; after all, we tend not to believe that pigs can fly. *Third*, we must ask whether the beliefs we hold can be lived out in practice. Whereas the first two points are generally recognized, the third point is often missed. Many people hold beliefs in theory that they deny in practice. Where this happens, it is a clue that something is amiss.

We all have a faith. I am a Christian because I consider Christianity to be the most reasonable faith. In the rest of the book, I will attempt to explain why.

SECTION 1.1

EXAMINING LIFE

Our Knowledge of the World

1

BECAUSE THERE IS SOMETHING RATHER THAN NOTHING

Take a look around the room. Pick an object. Now, ask yourself whether or not that object must exist—or is it possible for that object not to exist? Follow the same process for a couple of other objects. When we do this, we quickly recognize that everything we can see is *contingent*, by which I mean, it does not *have* to exist. In fact, we can probably remember or imagine the time when it did *not* exist. My house did not stand one hundred years ago; its bricks were not formed. The computer I use to write this exists now, but it did not do so a decade ago. I might reflect on myself: I do not have to exist; it is entirely possible for me not to exist. In fact, like all contingent things, there was a time when I did not exist. Think through as many examples as you like. You will see that in every case, the object of which you conceive is contingent and there was a time when it did not exist. This is always true: contingent objects or beings once did not exist.

The mystery of existence

And yet we exist. My computer exists. The world exists. This needs explaining—for as we saw in the last paragraph, none of these things have to exist, and *there was a time when none of them did exist*; so why do they exist now? What is the most reasonable explanation for that fact? We should add one more observation before we consider the possible answers: not only does the universe exist, but what exists includes beings of immense complexity—beings who are *personal*. By personal, I mean that we are beings with consciousness: the ability to enjoy a sense of self, to have individual meaning and purpose, and to exercise choice. Human beings have always observed themselves to be different from *impersonal* beings and always live as if this is true.

We are contingent beings in a universe of entirely contingent things, and our existence is marked by immense complexity and by personality. As we saw earlier, none of this has to be the case; it is entirely possible for everything not to exist. But it does exist. The question we face is this: "Why is there personal existence in a complex universe, rather than nothing at all?" What is the most reasonable belief to hold? At the most basic level, there are only three possible answers to this question. What exists either came out of (1) nothing, (2) impersonal existence, or (3) personal existence. Let's take each of these in turn and see which seems most reasonable.

Existence from nothing?

Is it reasonable to think that what exists came out of nothing? For this to be the case, we have to start with absolutely nothing. No matter, energy, or beings of any kind. Imagine that the universe was a completely empty room—and then take away the room! Although we cannot prove this to be impossible, I have never met anyone who believes this to be the case, and for good reason. All our experience tells us that nothing comes out of nothing—that if something begins to exist, it does so because something else has (in some way) brought it into existence. Just as in mathematics you can multiply zero as many times as you like and the answer will still be zero, so, too, with existence. Nothing will always produce nothing.

Existence from the impersonal?

The second possibility is that all that now exists comes out of impersonal existence (for example, matter or physical forces), that there is some raw material out of which everything that now exists has developed. It doesn't really matter *what* this beginning is made up of, the key point is that it is impersonal—merely a set of physical raw materials. Is this a reasonable explanation for why we now exist in the kind of universe in which we exist? It seems to me that there are two problems with this.

First, if there is an impersonal beginning, there seems no explanation of why the universe has developed into complex personal life. What I mean is this: why did the universe not remain as basic impersonal materials? There is nothing to make decisions about the development of the universe; there is nothing with a sense of purpose or direction, because those are functions of *persons*, and we are talking about an impersonal beginning. All that you have is the raw material, chance, and time. But time and chance guarantee nothing; they do not lead to all imaginable outcomes. This seems to me to be a problem: how can the impersonal ever produce the complexity and personality of human beings? It's important to remember that in this explanation we have only impersonal materials. We cannot start talking as if the development of complex life forms were inevitable, for that implies a sense of purpose or of direction, but impersonal matter and energy have neither.

Second, if all that exists comes from the impersonal, then it is hard to see why anything that exists is meaningful. We are just the outcome of the random processes of material physical properties over a period of time. Nothing more. For sure, this is not a logical problem in the same way the last point is; but as I pointed out in the introduction, one way we test whether our beliefs are reasonable is by seeing whether we can live them out. I have met people who claim that they believe we are the meaningless, random outcome of impersonal raw materials, but I have not yet met anyone who can live as if that were true.

Existence from the personal?

This leaves us with our final option, that our contingent universe came out of personal existence. What I mean is that there is an ultimate reality that produced, and in some way stands behind, the material universe. Any such reality must, logically, be of a fundamentally different nature to the material universe, and this ultimate reality must be personal (because only persons can *choose* to create). This is what we speak of when we speak of God. If this is the case, we have a sufficient explanation for the complexity of the universe, and we have a sufficient explanation for the existence of personal beings. Not only that, but we have an explanation for our sense of meaning and purpose, as we will come to in a later chapter. This cannot be proved absolutely—none of our three options can—but it seems to me to be the most reasonable.

In summary then, I am a Christian because I find the most reasonable belief as to why there is something complex and personal, rather than nothing, is that our existence comes from a personal beginning—one who *created* the existence we currently experience—which is exactly what Christianity claims.

2

BECAUSE OF SCIENCE

"I don't have a faith, I'm more a science kind of person." How many times have you heard (or perhaps said) sentences like that? I have heard it several times. As we discussed in the introduction to the book, the truth is that everybody operates with faith and with reason, but the old (supposed) polarity between faith and science is still alive and well for many people. I find this ironic, because modern science is one of the reasons that I am a Christian.

The development of science

Pause for a moment to think about this: why was it that in Europe empiricism and science blossomed? After all, many cultures explored the material world and grew in knowledge of it. Some pursued forms of astrology, magic, and healing; others achieved great feats of engineering, complex calendrical systems, or progressive medical practices; but none of them developed into what we now know as modern science. One (perhaps surprising) part of answer is that it was because Europe was *Christian* through the Middle Ages and into the modern period. Christian theology established a worldview that led to the development of science. To see why requires a little imagination . . .

Science works only on the basis that there is an order to the universe that allows it to be regular, predictable, and rational. Take, for example, the fact that water always boils at one hundred degrees and freezes at zero. If every time you heated up water, it boiled at different temperatures, science would be impossible. Science relies on an ordered world that we are able to understand. Now, what requires imagination is that *this has not always been the assumption*. Not all cultures in history have assumed that the universe is rational and its order is discoverable. After all, why should it be? Why should we believe that discoveries can be made that tell us something true about the way the universe works? Even if such laws existed, why should we think that we would be able to understand them? For science to have developed, humanity needed a cultural context in which such beliefs seemed plausible, and this was provided, in Europe, by theism. Theism is the claim that the universe was created by a rational God who had also created rational humanity, which led to the scientific impulse. As the historian Rodney Stark puts it: "It was only because Europeans believed in God as the intelligent designer of a rational universe that they pursued the secrets of creation."[1] Stark demonstrates that out of fifty-two leading scientists between 1543 and 1680 (the period of Copernicus and the rise of modern science), only one could be called a skeptic; the others were people of Christian faith.

"Fair enough," we may say, "but we no longer need Christianity to pursue science. Don't the discoveries of science themselves disagree with Christianity?" Well, I have never found this to be the case when we take a responsible and informed approach to both science and Christianity. In fact, there are two aspects of science that I find make Christianity more plausible.

The "faith" of the scientist

For anyone to conduct scientific study, one needs to hold two beliefs: first, that the world one is studying is ordered and stable

1. Rodney Stark, *The Triumph of Christianity* (New York: HarperCollins, 2012), 287.

enough to be understood; and second, that our minds can understand it. We all live as if these beliefs are true, but the point I want to highlight is that these are *beliefs*. We do not arrive at those conclusions after we have conducted our experiments; they are the presuppositions that we have to hold in order to do any experiments at all. As David Bentley Hart puts it:

> Sciences continue in their very different ways to discover
> ever deeper layers of intelligibility, and both [biology and
> physics] are inspired by a faith in the rational lawfulness
> of nature, and in the power of conceptual paradigms to
> reflect the rational truths on which reality is built.[2]

What is the most reasonable explanation for those beliefs? It is possible to say that we are justified to hold those beliefs because science "works"—we believe the universe is rational, because we find that it is rational—and this is surely true and presumably enough for some people. But I find that this is not a fully satisfying explanation. I may discover through experience my universe is understandable, but this does not help me to grasp *why* this is the case. At this point, I am either left asking questions about God, or I must stop asking questions altogether.

What we discover through science

As we act on our beliefs by pursuing scientific investigation, we grow in our knowledge of the world in which we live. What we discover invites us to make *interpretations*: how are we to make sense of what science shows us? In particular, what are we to make of the precision, order, and beauty of the world we discover through scientific investigation? We might take, for example, some of the basic physical laws that control everything in the universe, including the universe's development (like the ratio of electromagnetic force to the force of gravity). Several of these fundamental constants were analyzed by Sir Martin Rees, the former president

2. David Bentley Hart, *The Experience of God* (New Haven, CT: Yale University Press, 2013), 232.

of the Royal Society of London, when Rees argued that if any of these fundamental constants was slightly different, human life as we have it would be impossible. But there is no necessary scientific reason why these constants must be as they are. How might we interpret such precision? If we wish to think that there is no personal being that somehow stands behind our physical universe, we must in the end conclude that all such realities are random, not in the sense that they are disordered but that there is no meaning to them. In a similar way, evolution is often described as a random process, but as the Oxford and Princeton scientists Andrew Briggs, Hans Halvorson, and Andrew Steane write:

> Randomness is not the dominant principle in evolution ... when one looks into it, one finds that the structure in biology is far from a fluke. The shape of living things is largely owing to profound harmony deep in the nature of the physical world ... including mathematical and physical and chemical and also extending into the patterns of social relations.[3]

Of course, none of this proves that God exists, but we must ask what is most reasonable, both in justifying our scientific faith and in making sense of our discoveries. We must remember that if there is only our material universe, then all we have discussed is the result of undirected chemical and physical processes, and we should expect a world that reflects this narrative—one devoid of purpose and essentially random. But is this the kind of world in which we live? It seems, instead, that science shows us a very different kind of universe, and our scientific endeavors require us to hold beliefs about an ordered universe we can understand. How we explain *that* is the real question about the relationship between faith and science. I consider Christianity reasonable because it provides a robust answer to those questions: the existence of an ordered, precise, rational, and beautiful universe, which correlates with our minds points to a personal origin for both—a God that

---

3. Andrew Briggs, Hans Halvorson, and Andrew Steane, *It Keeps Me Seeking: The Invitation from Science, Philosophy, and Religion* (Oxford, UK: Oxford University Press, 2018), 203.

stands behind the physical universe and our consciousness that is able to appreciate it.

3

Because Things Happen

O f all the reasons I give in this book as to why I am a Christian, this is perhaps the one that is most difficult to understand— it will require concentration! If we can stay with the argument, though, it is worth the effort. The starting point is something we all take for granted: causes. Think about any event (something that happens) or any condition (something that is): both rely on a previous set of conditions and events. In some ways, this is similar to thinking about contingent things (which we discussed in chapter 1); the difference is that in this chapter, I would like to think more about causes and effects.

Why anything happens

To take an example close to my heart—Manchester United won the treble in 1999 with two goals in the closing minutes of the Champions League final. That event occurred only because other events had occurred (purchasing Teddy Sheringham, or employing Alex Ferguson as manager, for example). It also occurred because of prior conditions (the physical environment necessary for football and human existence). Without previous causal conditions and events, that particular event would not have happened. You can think of your own examples and how they depend on previous causal conditions. If we do this enough, we come to recognize that *nothing occurs in our physical existence that does not have previous causal conditions.* If we take these observations to their logical conclusion, we have a reason to believe in God's existence.

First, we must understand that what we have just described is a causal series. One event or condition leads to a further event or condition and so on. Dallas Willard invites us to imagine this as a row of dominoes. Each domino that falls (an event or condition) does so because the one before it has fallen. This means that there must be a first domino—a beginning of the causal series. Willard explains why this is the case:

> You have a line of dominoes standing on end in such a way that if one is pushed over, it knocks over the next one in the direction it falls, and so on down the line. Now imagine a line of dominoes falling toward your right and a line of those already having fallen disappearing over the horizon to your left. Someone suggests to you that the line to your left has no first member. They are saying that for every domino in the sequence to your left there is another fallen domino beyond it to your left, which made it fall. That is to say, the sequence of falling dominoes leading up to this one now falling right before you is *unlimited*, infinite, with no first member . . . . But if there were no first domino to fall, not knocked over by another domino, there would be no last one before *this* one, to make this one fall, and so it would not fall. But it does fall. There is such a last one, so there is a first domino to fall. If there were no first domino to fall, the sequence of falling dominoes to the left would be unlimited or infinite, and it would never "reach" the domino that, just having fallen, knocks over the one falling here and now in front of you.[1]

1. Dallas Willard, *Knowing Christ Today: Why We Can Trust Spiritual Knowledge* (San Francisco: HarperCollins, 2009), 105.

The necessity of a beginning

The trouble we have is that it is very difficult for us to distinguish forever (or infinitity, eternality) and a really long time. It is entirely possible to argue that the causal series goes on for a really long time; it is illogical to argue that it goes on forever. If it were truly infinite, nothing would be happening now, because we would never have got here. So it cannot have gone on forever. So there must have been a beginning.

And—breathe! This is difficult stuff (can any of us really conceive of infinity very well?), but there is only one more step to go. If there is a beginning, a first cause (or first domino), then it *cannot be a merely physical beginning*. That is because, as we have already seen, everything physical depends on prior causal conditions. If the beginning were just another physical event or condition, then it would still be stuck inside the row of dominos. This means that the beginning must be *outside* the row of dominos. It must be a different kind of entity—that is, what we call God.

Putting it together

I will summarize twice, once with dominoes and once without.

The dominoes that are falling now have been knocked over by previous dominoes. This cannot have gone on forever, because if it had, then the dominoes in front of us would not be falling over, because forever would never reach now. Therefore, there must be a first domino. That first domino must *not* have depended on a previous domino to fall over (otherwise it would not be the first), so the first domino must be a very different kind of domino.

Everything that happens does so because of previous causal conditions and events. This cannot have gone on forever; there must be a beginning. This beginning point cannot be another physical event or condition but must be a non-physical beginning, i.e., God.

So where does this leave us? Well, for a start, it does not tell us very much about God, other than a few important things: that God stands behind the physical order, that God is not caused in the way that everything else is, that God is capable of creating the physical existence we know, and that God is personal. God has chosen to create what now exists, so God must be, in some sense, a person who makes choices.

Some of us are more comfortable with abstract thought than others, but I hope most of you who read this book can make sense of this chapter. If not, I trust you will get more out of the others. If this does make sense to us, we must consider the consequences of this argument. It seems to me that the only way to deny the existence of God is to deny the causal series—that is, to claim that what we observe and conceive of as cause and effect is somehow incorrect. Some philosophers in history have done exactly that. The question then is which is a more reasonable belief: the argument I have just offered or a denial of cause and effect? We all like to be right, so we all tend towards the argument that gives us the result we want; but if we want to know what is true, we must attempt to resist that and consider these beliefs against the criteria we outlined at the start of the book.

I am a Christian because things happen. And if things happen, there must have been a first cause that is non-physical. This seems to me logically secure and internally coherent and is a belief that is livable. I am not convinced the same can be said for a set of beliefs that denies cause and effect.

SECTION 1.2

EXAMINING LIFE

Our Knowledge of Ourselves

4

BECAUSE OF OUR NEED FOR LOVE

There are some things in life that we all experience wherever and whenever we live, no matter what culture we are a part of. They are undeniable. However, it is easy to avoid giving much thought to this; we rarely *examine* our lives and think about how to make sense of our common experience. In this and the following two chapters I want to probe three of these areas, because I find these common experiences to be among the biggest clues to the existence of God and the truth of Christianity. Let's start with love.

Our need for love

We all need love. This is one of the most obvious statements about humanity that can be made. From the moment we are born, we crave the comfort and care of our parents, and small babies quickly die without them. In those around us at every stage of life, we can observe the need for belonging, approval, affirmation, physical touch, friendship . . . in short, for love. You know this subjectively. Examine your own life, choices, and desires; you, too, are deeply controlled by the need to love and be loved. In fact, those humans who shy away from love we usually consider broken or ill in some way, in a condition that needs repairing. Psychotherapists tell us that love is the foundation of the human sense of self and of the creation of identity. A glance into culture tells us that much human self-expression focusses on love or its complications. History confirms that this has always been the case. Somewhere deep in our gut, we know that love is the answer to all our problems and the center of all our pleasures. Humans need to love and to be loved.

Our need for perfect love

But we can go further. We do not just want love. Our common human experience tells us that we crave *perfect love*. This is part of the problem of the human condition—you see, no matter how good any particular expression of love that touches us is, it is never quite all that we want and need. This truth is something we tend to avoid, but if we risk thinking about it and looking deeply into our own experience, we know that it is true. Hollywood makes millions of dollars each year telling us that if we could meet the perfect partner, we would find true love, which satisfies all our desires. Well, I have yet to find a real person for whom this is the case! Wonderful as my own wife is, she is unable to meet all my needs for love or satisfy me completely. The same will be true for you with your partner, *and it will be true for every human relationship.* I deeply love my children, but I know that my love is not always enough for them. They want more than I can give. When we have a fantastic group of friends, there will always be times we still feel lonely or misunderstood. The best sex still cannot take away the feeling that, somehow, there must be more than this. All these moments of real love that we experience are good, but they are also bittersweet. When we experience them, it is like we reach beyond them for something more, but it slips through our fingers.

Why should this be the case? Why, when we spend so much of our time and energy giving and receiving love, should we find we still need more? What is the most reasonable way to explain the human need for love that seems insatiable? Which beliefs best make sense of this? This is an important question, for unless we make sense of our need for love, we are at risk of always living on the edge of despair. Many relationships end because people are looking for a perfect love they can never find. Many of us endlessly distract ourselves with food, drink, entertainment, work, etc., because when we have a quiet moment, we feel our inner need for love rising up and have no idea how to satisfy it.

Possible explanations

Some attempt to explain this by appeal to our evolutionary history. This approach is usually associated with naturalism—the belief that there is nothing supernatural in the world and that what is meaningful is that which can be explained by science. This world-view suggests that what we call love is a disposition that causes us to behave in certain ways—to reproduce, protect our families, and solidify our communities. It might be further suggested that our strong desire for love has given us evolutionary advantage, and our successful survival is, in part, an accident of this inherited impulse. So to the question "Why do we desire perfect love?" some might reply, "Because that random development in your evolutionary history has proved to be useful."

It is initially worth noticing that this is less of an explanation (answering the why question) than a description. Yes, it may be true that our desire for love has played out in these ways, but that does not explain its origin or even its possibility as an evolutionary development. I imagine naturalists would have to say that it just emerged at some point (but how and why?). In any case, this account of love seems highly reductionistic. Our desire for love longs for more than the achievement of survival. As discussed above, even when we are immersed in meaningful relationships, our need for love is not quenched. It may be helpful to compare it to our physical hunger. When I am hungry, I eat, feel full, and no longer want to eat. However, when I desire love, though I experience love, I still ache for more. Nor can the naturalist narrative explain the need for humans to express their desires in art, music, and all manner of creative media that have nothing at all to contribute to our survival.

A different (more Eastern) approach is to claim that the desire for love is an inappropriate attachment to the world that we need to transcend; we should free ourselves from this need for love. This too seems implausible. It is love that pushes us towards our greatest moments and best actions. This need for love is the center of healthy human existence. As psychologists have shown, the denial of love early in life can have catastrophic consequences for a person, which are often never overcome in the rest of life. To deny the need for love seems comparable to denying the need for water; I have never seen anyone able to actually live this out in practice.

There is a more rationally plausible option: that our need for a *perfect* love is because we were created by a person who is the origin and essence of perfect love. We were made for love, and the reason we cannot find all the love we were made for in other people is because we were made for a love that is greater than human love; we were made for the perfect love of God. Why else would every human have this need? Why else would we be unable to find a love that is satisfied in each other? One of Christianity's central claims is that God *is* love. God is its definition, origin, and consummation. The good love we experience slips through our fingers because it points to the God who is the only ultimate source of the love we need.

So I am a Christian because we all need a perfect love that none of us can find, which points to the reasonable belief that we were made for the perfect love of God.

5

BECAUSE OF OUR EXPERIENCE OF MORALITY

As with love, so with morality—we all know what it is to feel a sense of right and wrong. When was the last time someone pushed into a queue in which you were standing? Do you remember the anger you felt? When was the last time you were lied to by a colleague? What about the last time you lied to someone else? Does your conscience not twinge as you recall the incident? Our morality is normal, demonstrated by the fact that those who do not seem to have a functioning moral compass are often sectioned and given psychological care. The question, though, is how we can explain our common morality. There is much that has been said, but I want to focus on one issue in particular, the problem of objective morality.

Objective morality

It used to be the case that everyone thought that there was a right and a wrong that were true for everyone (this is what I mean by objective morality, that if something is wrong, it is wrong for everyone). Two hundred years ago, I would sit in the pub banging my pint on the table, arguing with you about whether it was right or not for me to have an affair, or for you to lie to the government about your taxes. We may disagree on *what is right* (e.g., I may think an affair is fine, you may think it is wrong), but what we would agree about is that *there is a right*. If it is right for me, it must also be right for you, because right is right.

Now, however, we live in a different age. We can talk about affairs and conclude that there is no right and wrong in the objective sense but only what is "right for me." This is postmodern pluralism in the realm of ethics: there are no ethical standards that are more authoritative than my own conviction. Abortion? Theft? Lying? How I spend my money? Drugs? With whom I have sex? In all these areas, there are no absolutes now, there is just what is right for me. You may not have thought about this so clearly before, but I expect that subconsciously this is also your assumption. To prove it to yourself, just imagine that someone told you that your current relationship was immoral. I imagine your internal response runs along these lines: "What a ridiculous thing to say. How dare this person question my decisions like that? It's my freedom and my life. How can a private relationship be immoral? They may feel it is wrong because of their own opinions, but I'm not them. It's fine for me." That's a toned-down version—our reactions are often more strongly worded! In short, we are now wired to think that morality is a matter of personal choice.

A *matter of opinion?*

Or are we? Although in some areas we think like this, I have never met anyone able to live like this in the whole of life. If morality were only a matter of my opinion, then there is no ultimate reason why we should disapprove of wealthy people avoiding tax. Why is that immoral? If we respond that they are breaking the law, we may reply, "What's wrong with breaking the law?" If they want to do that and feel okay about it, there is no ultimate reason I can give them as to why their behavior is wrong. Or to take an even more provocative example, what about those who are sexually attracted to children and want to act on those impulses? What makes this ultimately *wrong*? If we reply that it harms children, they may respond either by saying that there are some children who would not be harmed, or, to go further, they may ask why some children should not be harmed. What makes that ultimately wrong? When we cry injustice—that something is not fair—then the response again can be "Why should it be fair?" (We will come to the issue of justice in another chapter.)

Do you see the problem? If right and wrong are just a matter of opinion, then all we can do, ultimately, is scream, "I don't like it!" There is nothing more. But I have never met anyone who can live like this. We all feel that right and wrong are more than this—that there are some actions that are *always* right and *always* wrong. We should see, then, that many of us live in contradiction. We say *in theory* that morals are relative (and apply our theory in some areas), but we all *actually* think that it is never okay to kill an innocent victim and it is always right to save a dying child. In the end, none of us is willing to believe morality is relative; we cannot live consistently with our apparent beliefs. But if there *is* some objective morality, there has to be a moral authority that is greater than my opinion or yours. There has to be some way of defining right and wrong that's bigger than me or you.

Responding to the puzzle

For naturalists, perhaps the most common approach is to claim that our ethical impulse is, again, merely an evolutionary development that has turned out to be advantageous; our survival as a species can be correlated to our desire to help others and do what is commonly conceived as right. Again, though, this is not really an explanation but only a description. It has nothing to say about why we are moral but only comments on the advantages of being moral. It does not explain the existence of morality as an evolutionary option in the first place.

The most significant problem with this worldview, though, is that although it may have something to say about how our current morality has developed, it fails as an attempt to give us an objective basis for *what is* right and wrong. If what we formerly considered right behavior were no longer beneficial to survival, there is no reason we should not redefine what is right. If the best thing for our species' survival were to wipe out all the over-70s in the country, I do not see how we can conclude that this is wrong from the naturalist perspective. It may explain why I *feel* it is wrong, but it cannot tell me that it *is* wrong. I am left only with a relative morality. If we are naturalists, then, we must accept that we have an impulse (that morality is objective) that we cannot justify. I may feel things are right and wrong, but that is simply my feeling and nothing more. Ultimately, those who have a different moral opinion from me may be equally right, even if I find their choices distasteful.

A second kind of explanation is to claim that our sense of objective morality is because we were created by a moral being. That is, we feel a sense of right and wrong because morality is connected to the very foundations of existence. What is right and wrong is connected to the good intentions God has for his creation—to know love, joy, beauty, happiness, and so on. So morality is objective, both because it is related to what actually exists and because it comes from a moral authority beyond me or you. Christians claim that we are made in the image of God; part of being in his image is sharing in his moral nature. We know in our guts that there is a right and a wrong because of who made us. We feel that some things are right *because they are right.*

I am a Christian because we share a common experience of objective morality. When we examine which narrative is able to best make sense of our common moral intuitions, I find it is belief in a moral creator that provides the most coherent explanation of our experience and gives us rational grounds for believing morality to be objective rather than relative.

6

BECAUSE OF OUR UNFULFILLED DESIRES

P hilosophers throughout history have observed that humans aim for happiness. In every decision, people always choose what they think will lead to their greatest happiness (although we are often mistaken). One of the greatest puzzles of our existence, then, is why we cannot find the happiness we are looking for. The nineteenth-century poet Matthew Arnold beautifully describes this feeling in his poem *The Buried Life*:

> But often, in the world's most crowded streets,
> But often, in the din of strife,
> There rises an unspeakable desire
> After the knowledge of our buried life;
> A thirst to spend our fire and restless force
> In tracking out our true, original course;
> A longing to inquire
> Into the mystery of this heart which beats
> So wild, so deep in us—to know
> Whence our lives come and where they go.

No matter what we do with our lives, the happiness we seek seems so temporary, so elusive. It is, like Arnold says, as if we are search-ing for a buried life—one that we are aware of but is forever just out of reach. The seventeenth-century French intellectual Blaise Pascal wrote this:

> All men seek happiness. There are no exceptions. However different the means they may employ, they all strive towards this goal . . . . Yet for very many years no one without faith has ever reached the goal at which everyone is continually aiming . . . . What else does this craving, and this helplessness, proclaim but that there was once in man a true happiness, of which all that now remains is the empty print and tract?[1]

The happiness we cannot find

Many of us avoid thinking about this issue because to do so is both painful and unnerving. Dare we really contemplate our own unhappiness? I am not claiming that we are never happy; that is evidently false. There are many joys in life that we will experience and many times where we taste genuine happiness. The problem is that these experiences are so transient; our true moments of joy slip away almost as soon as we realize how happy we are. No matter how much good we are given in life, we ache for more. We do not, I think, want something totally different from the happiness we experience, but we want a happiness that has a substance or permanence that is more real than we currently know.

I hope that doesn't sound too mystical—it is hard to articulate such feelings—but if we are honest with ourselves, I suspect we can all identify with what I am describing. It is most recognizable when it occurs in the midst of the thing in which we have put our hope: if I have convinced myself that having a big, healthy family will make me happy, why is it that I can sit around the Christmas tree with my wife and children yet still feel unfulfilled? If I have believed that achievement will make me happy, why is it that it never does? The Hollywood film star Jim Carrey is quoted as saying, "I

---

1. Blaise Pascal, *Pensées*, translated by A. J. Krailsheimer (London: Penguin, 1995), 45.

think everybody should get rich and famous and do everything they ever dreamed of so they can see that it's not the answer." I wonder what it is for you?

How might we explain this? Why is it that we all pursue happiness, but the happiness we find never completely fills the internal void? Why do we keep imagining that the next thing will do the trick, when nothing so far has been enough?

It seems to me there are only two conclusions we might draw from all this. Either our felt desire for happiness is realistic—that is, it is a desire that is rational and has the possibility of fulfilment—or it is illusory—that is, it is a mistake or defect that plagues the human race with an irrational and futile desire that can never be satisfied. These are surely the only two basic options.

A futile pursuit?

Let's take the second option first. It is surely a logical possibility that such desires are defective. Perhaps they are meaningless leftovers from our evolutionary history where such desires helped us to survive; perhaps they are just the psychological reality of being human—the random outcome of the physical processes that constitute our material existence. In such a situation, or others like it, it seems to me the only rational conclusion is that our desire for happiness must be denied. It can never be satisfied, as there is no greater happiness than what we can experience now; if this doesn't do the job, there is nothing else. The best way forward is to eradicate these desires and settle for whatever happiness comes our way. This is the approach of much Eastern spirituality (and a fair amount of classical Western philosophy): become detached from your desires in order to be liberated from them.

If that is correct, then we must stop pursuing the happiness we desire (as it is unattainable), embrace nihilism, and attempt to enjoy what is available to us—settle for less, rather than live a forever-disappointed quest for more. This certainly seems an internally consistent belief to hold, but like other issues this book raises, my experience is that it is difficult to find people who actually *live* like this is what they believe. As Alexander Pope wrote: "Hope springs eternal in the human breast." We cannot seem to let go of our desire for happiness, even if our worldview tells us we should. If our desires are unattainable, then suicide is increasingly logical (as some Western philosophical traditions have recognized). The fact we continue to consider suicide as tragic indicates that we do not really accept this. It seems to me, then, that this worldview is unlivable and that most of those who say they believe it live in contradiction between their actions and their beliefs. This should suggest to us that it may not be the most reasonable set of beliefs to hold.

The pleasures of God

The other option is that our desires for happiness are realistic but the reason they are unfulfilled is that they cannot be *entirely* fulfilled by physical pleasures and human relationships. These are good things, for sure, but they are not enough, because we were made for a greater happiness. To return to Pascal:

> This [void] he tries in vain to fill with everything around him, seeking in things that are not there the help he cannot find in those that are, though none can help, since this infinite abyss can be filled only with an infinite and immutable object; in other words by God himself.[2]

C. S. Lewis became a Christian partly because he realized that he was designed for a joy he could not yet fully grasp. His own experience told him that there must be more—that he was called beyond what he currently knew, into a happiness that he had experienced in part but not yet in full. This is exactly what the Christian narrative claims we should expect: the desire for happiness is there, because we were all created by God who designed us to know him and find our happiness in relationship to him. We experience much happiness through our material world and relationships with others, because these were created by God to give

2. Pascal, *Pensées*, 45.

us pleasure, but they cannot *fully* meet our need for happiness, because it is only ultimately satisfied in God himself. It is true to say we long for a *divine* happiness, not totally unlike the happiness we have tasted, but deeper, fuller, and infinite.

So I am a Christian because we all long for a happiness we cannot find, and this tells us we were made for a greater happiness that can be found only in God. No other narrative gives an explanation of our common experience that I find to be as coherent or as livable.

SECTION 1.3

EXAMINING LIFE

Our Common Human Behavior

7

BECAUSE WE ENJOY BEAUTY

There are some parts of our lives that are so familiar, we over-look just how strange they really are. Or, perhaps better put, some aspects of human experience are so taken for granted that we do not often think about whether our worldview is sufficient to explain them or recognize their importance for making sense of life. We will explore five of these in this section. This chapter examines the phenomenon of beauty.

The experience of beauty

We all know what it is to be struck by beauty. Whether it is a sunset over the mountains, the smile of a baby, a walk through the forest, or a striking piece of architecture, we have all had times where we are confronted by something that compels us to say, internally or externally, "How beautiful is this!" Yet when we examine these experiences, their oddity demands an explanation. I have in mind two aspects of our experience:

First, beauty moves the soul. Or, at least, that is the best way I can put the inarticulable internal impact of experiencing what is beautiful. When we are confronted with the panoramic beauty of our world, when we sit on the beach late at night listening to the waves lapping the shore, something inside us is stirred. Something in us moves in response to the beauty we experience; we *feel more alive*.

Second, the experience of beauty has an excess, by which I mean, it always seems to *reach beyond* the thing we perceive to be beautiful. When I read that poem or hear that piece of music, what is awakened inside me is a desire, joy, aliveness that seems to be about more than the specific thing that began this experience. When I am moved to tears by a poem, if you were to ask me what it was about the poem that moved me, although I might point to one or two things in particular, the poem itself does not seem to be the whole story. It has pointed to something I cannot quite grasp, and it is this *beauty beyond* the poem that is affecting me. When you gaze at the sunset, is the rapturous experience of beauty sufficiently explained by the sunset alone? I do not think it is. The effect beauty has on us regularly goes beyond the things in themselves.

The oddness of beauty

Is there not something quite odd about all that I have just described? Why should I have an intense desire for something that is not satisfied when I gain that experience? If I am hungry, a good meal usually leaves me content, but the desire for beauty is not quite like that. Beauty causes us to long for something that goes beyond the object we consider beautiful; it seems to wake our imagination, but we cannot quite put into words what we are trying to imagine.

All of this makes beauty a bit of a problem for worldviews shaped by naturalism, for beauty is quite resistant to being explained in reductionistic terms. Do we find such beauty in the natural world simply because these landscapes were desirable at some earlier point in our evolutionary development? Is all that we find beautiful explicable as related to some survival need in the distant past? Such explanations seem to strain credulity as a sufficient explanation for our experience of beauty, because there is always an *excess*, something so *unnecessary* that these kinds of arguments can never account for. Why are we not content simply to eat food that provides us with the nutrition we need, rather than enjoying the pleasure of something that tastes wonderful in addition? Any account of beauty that attempts to say "beauty is just . . ." fails to explain why so many of us experience beauty as somehow speaking to us (finding music to be meaningful, for example) or why we experience it pointing beyond itself, in the way I described above.

So what does beauty point to? Why is it we come alive in the presence of beauty? I guess it is possible to say that all these feelings are a common human error and that beauty points to nothing at all; it is meaningless, and all I have described is to desire nothing but an illusion. And yet, many of us have discovered that as we pursue our longings, we do indeed find something. Or someone.

The meaning of beauty

Beauty points beyond itself, and what it points to is what Christians call God. I do not know what you think of when you think of God, but one way to begin understanding what Christians mean is to think of God as the origin of all beauty and the full satisfaction of the kind of desires we have when we enjoy something beautiful. For Christians, we can explain the excess of beauty by seeing that all beauty does indeed point beyond itself—to the infinite beauty of God who is partly manifested in each particular experience of beauty that we may have. That is why for the Christian, as we plunge deeper into beauty, we experience more of God; and as we grow in knowing God, we experience ever deeper beauty. That may not be the way you have been used to thinking of God, but it is not a bad place to start. If we want to reject this worldview, we must come up with a reasonable alternative to explain what beauty points to and why it awakens such life within us.

In his novel *The Pilgrim's Regress*, C. S. Lewis presents an extended allegory for making sense of life, surveying the different worldview options one may encounter along the way. Interestingly, he begins his narrative of the search for meaning by describing the vision of an island. The pilgrim of his story feels an intense desire for that island, and it is this that keeps him moving from one worldview to another, each offering to satisfy the desires awakened by the island, but all of them failing to do so, until he comes to Christianity. Lewis was extremely rational and of outstanding intellect. He spent years being trained in dialectic (logical argument) and was academically and personally familiar with the major worldview options. And yet it was the ineffable experience of beauty that forced him to confront the inadequacy of a worldview without God; he found his experience simply could not be explained or satisfied within a naturalist worldview. The reason we so deeply desire beauty is not because of some material need to which beauty is related but because we were created by a God of infinite beauty, to enjoy the beauty of who he is. Infinitely.

So, like Lewis, I am a Christian because of my experience of beauty. I find that it calls me to a greater pleasure beyond the beauty I experience, and I find the most reasonable explanation for this is that of the Christian narrative, that my experiences are a taste of the infinite beauty of God, from whom I ultimately come and towards whom my desires are ultimately directed.

8

Because of Our Sense of Justice

"It's not fair!" Our sense of justice is not only one of the most common human experiences but is also one that is most important to us. It moves us to action. It makes and breaks relationships. It pushes us to joy or despair. For some, the desire for justice shapes much of their lives. It is surely one of our deepest instincts. Go to any school playground, and within a few minutes, you are likely to hear arguments about what is or is not fair. It provokes strong emotions in us. We all know the surge of rage when we believe we have been treated unjustly. We can see our desire for justice on a communal level in the sheer amount of money and time we plough into our justice system and our declarations that everybody has the right to a fair trial or to be otherwise protected by the law. Where does our sense of justice come from, and how might we explain its power? But that is only one of the pressing questions our sense of justice puts to us. The other is more disturbing: why is it that despite such a common and deep desire for justice, there is so much injustice in our lives?

Greatness and wretchedness

For a community of people who seem to care so much about justice, we see an awful lot of injustice going on, at every level of our society. Powerful nations exploit smaller ones; powerful individuals live beyond the reach of the courts. The rich get richer, and the poor get poorer. The innocent are convicted, and the guilty walk away laughing. In our own families and friendships, we can treat one another unfairly, despite our common desire for justice. This is even true of those we tend to think of as good people. Most of those who choose to work for charities do so because they have a strong desire to make a difference in the world—to advance the cause of justice and help others. But we have read in recent years about charity workers using child prostitutes whilst working to restore communities after the Boxing Day tsunami. The converse is also true: those we think of as evil often also desire justice in some form. Hitler, for example, passed several laws preventing cruelty to animals.

Blaise Pascal puts it well when he says this:

> Man's greatness and wretchedness are so evident that the true worldview must necessarily teach us that there is in man some great principle of greatness and some great principle of wretchedness and it must account for such amazing contradictions.[1]

How do we explain such a deep desire for justice and our continued inability to find it? How can we sacrifice so much for justice and yet continually fail to attain to our own standards? The British theologian Tom Wright puts it like this:

> We dream the dream of justice. We glimpse, for a moment, a world at one, a world put to rights, a world where things work out, where societies function healthily, where I not only know what I ought to do but actually do it. And then we wake up and come back to reality . . . isn't it strange that we should all want things to be put to rights but that we can't seem to do it? And isn't the oddest

1. Pascal, *Pensées*, 46.

thing the fact that I, myself, know what I ought to do but often don't do it![2]

Examining the contradiction

How do we make sense of these aspects of our common experience? For naturalists, perhaps the most common answer is that our sense of justice is both genetically inherited and shaped by our social conditioning as we grow up. Perhaps random at first, the instinct for justice has facilitated our evolutionary development, and we have now recognized that it is necessary to develop social rules that allow us to flourish, for the good of the species. These social rules are what we call justice, and they are ultimately a consequence of our evolutionary past.

This may be of some interest as a description of the impact of our sense of justice on evolutionary process, but it does not take us very far as an explanation of why our sense of justice is what it is, and it leaves us with multiple problems. I'll mention two. First, if we take this position to its logical conclusion, it seems that there is no good reason why we should not treat humans that are weaker unjustly. If justice is primarily about species survival, why should we not eradicate those whose genes are faulty or deficient, as was the case in the eugenics movement of the nineteenth and twentieth centuries? This was a deliberate decision to try to eradicate weaker genes from humanity by stopping certain humans from reproducing. Now, most reading this would find the idea that I could have children, but you might not be allowed to "because of your genes," as judged by me, to be unfair. Yet if justice is founded on species survival, then eugenics seems a logical conclusion. But we think it unjust. The second problem is that the naturalist explanation cannot explain why we fail so badly to live up to our ideals, for in this worldview, you would expect us to be getting better and better at justice. I am not convinced this is the case. Therefore, it seems

2. Tom Wright, *Simply Christian* (London: SPCK, 2006), 3, 8.

to me, naturalism struggles to explain either our greatness or our wretchedness.

Another approach is that taken by a fair amount of Eastern religion and philosophy. In the famous Hindu text the Bhagavad Gita, one of the central lessons is that humanity, the world, and the divine are ultimately indivisible. There are no friends or enemies, good or bad, justice or injustice; in the end, there is no moral differentiation, and our task is to accept the role in life we have been given and live it as it needs to be lived. In other words, our desire for justice is not something that needs explanation; it does not point to a problem to be solved or indicate a goal to pursue. The task is not to change our world but to escape it. It seems to me that this worldview essentially gives up the question of justice (and the questions Pascal posed), but I am unconvinced that humans can really live like this. Are we content to say our sense of justice is to desire an illusion? Can we really live accepting justice and injustice with an even hand? To do so seems to deny something at the core of who we are.

The Christian worldview takes neither of these paths but claims that we were made for relationships of love, and our sense of justice is so strong because justice is both "love in public" and incredibly beautiful. The desire is common because we are all made in the image of the beautiful, just, God of love. It also explains why we have a hard time reaching it, for the Christian narrative claims that, to some extent, we have each rejected God, who is the source of justice and gives the ability to act justly. This leaves us in a condition where we retain the desire for justice (greatness) but lack the power to achieve it (wretchedness). Christianity also tells the story of how justice will be restored and how part of our purpose is to participate in its restoration . . . but to flesh this out would take us too far away from our current focus (check the bibliography for some recommended books that do just that). For now, in summary, I am a Christian because I consider this narrative to be the most compelling explanation of our sense of justice.

9

BECAUSE WE LIVE AS IF WE CAN COMMUNICATE MEANINGFULLY

I am writing this book assuming that, as you read it, various thoughts that exist in my consciousness, which make claims about the world out there, will be understood by your consciousness in a way that is meaningful. That is, whether as a reader or a writer (or speaker or listener), we operate on the assumption that real communication about both our inner thoughts and some kind of reality outside ourselves is possible. We do this all the time, constantly believing ourselves to be communicating with one another and that such exchanges have meaning. It is so common that we rarely stop to think about how surprising it is that this should be possible or how we might explain this shared experience of the way language works and the beliefs that it entails.

Language and communication

We all assume that our language allows us to communicate with one another in a meaningful way, but we can also observe that our communication is never perfect. I trust that you can understand enough of my language to find this chapter meaningful, but I doubt whether you will perfectly receive my intended argument the way

I understand it. We are constantly clarifying and redescribing the things we try to talk about; we regularly misunderstand and work hard to better understand one another. There is something partial about our language in the sense that we never really finish communicating about anything. What we say is always incomplete or provisional—open to change and development. In summary, we might say that we all live making sense of the world with and to one another but that we never reach any finality. How might we make sense of our making sense in language?

It may be that our first reaction is to question whether there is anything here requiring an explanation. Can we not say that we have simply learned to communicate through practice as we have grown up; we have found that it works, and that is why we behave as we do? This may be correct, but that's not the real problem. What requires explaining is *why* it works. Why do my tools for making sense of the world in my consciousness correspond with your tools? Why do both of our tools seem to correspond with the world outside ourselves?

Consciousness and knowledge

To put it a different way, is it not astounding that the way my mind works (the categories in which it makes sense, generates understanding, orders my experiences) seems to fit with the world that I live in? Most of the time I do not find objects, creatures and experiences I encounter mysterious; I find them *intelligible*. And so do you. As we talk, we discover that there is a remarkable fit between our minds and our world, almost as if they were made for each other.

That being said, we do hit limits in our ability to comprehend, forcing differences in our assessments and opinions, leading to change and development in our understanding over time. Again, I write this book on the assumption that your way of making sense is open to future change, as is mine. I am writing and you are reading because this is always a shared enterprise between people, not an individual pursuit (after all, you would not even have language with which to think unless others had introduced you to language itself).

Finally, we may observe that all our communication operates with a trajectory; we want to know more, work stuff out, communicate more fully. Healthy human beings seem to believe that there is a world outside their consciousness to be known, that it is good to know it, that our language/communication is an essential means by which we do that, and that we never fully know, but there is always more to be said.

Making sense of making sense

Worldviews are themselves one name for our current beliefs, how we are making sense of our lives. The question is whether our current beliefs line up with our experience of language and communication. If we are naturalists, we will have to reject any explanation that does not start with impersonal material origins, and so the development of language and our experience of communication is often explained, like so many other things, as having its origins in evolutionary variation that, it turned out, enabled us to survive and continue to develop. Language is largely seen as instrumental—that is, it has its origin in serving functional purposes (like making known to others where food might be found).

Even if we would not want to reject every element of this narrative, it is hardly sufficient to make sense of all we have discussed in this chapter. Explaining the phenomenon of consciousness is hard enough for the naturalist (where and what exactly is the "I" that is the unifying perspective we experience?), never mind the remarkable way in which our consciousness coheres with the world beyond it. Moreover, the sheer richness of language—our ability to express so much in so many different ways—speaks of a desire to know and say more than is necessary in any functional sense. We make sense, but we also know there is much we do not know, so we reach for further knowledge of our world or one another, desiring something that is always partially discovered but never fully comprehended. It sounds a bit like what many mean by faith . . .

We find our world to be intelligible, which makes it reasonable to think that what is out there is inseparable from intelligence (or mind, consciousness, intentionality—whichever term you prefer). We all sense that there *is* something to know and to make sense of, and there is remarkable continuity in our attempts to do this over time. But what, or who, makes this possible? What intelligence is able to underwrite our language, to ensure we find our world intelligible and communication meaningful? As Rowan Williams puts it:

> These aspects of language seem to show that we live in an environment where intelligible communication is ubiquitous—where there is "sense" before we *make* sense.[1]

This is one of the things Christians mean when they refer to God—the one whose intelligence ensures the meaningfulness of our language and communication, our ability to make sense of the world and each other. This worldview tells us that our innate desire to know is because we were created to do so—that what is there is fundamentally good, and knowledge of it is to be desired. Our language is always provisional and incomplete not because it is faulty but because the God who stands behind it all is infinite. The task of making sense is endless but not hopeless. To touch on some themes in other chapters, the gift of language and communication is intimately connected with goodness, beauty, justice, and happiness—of which, according to this worldview, there is always more to be discovered.

So I am a Christian because I find this narrative can provide the most compelling explanation for our shared experience of language and communication.

---

1. Rowan Williams, *The Edge of Words: God and the Habits of Language* (London: Bloomsbury, 2014), 170.

10

Because We Live as If
There Is Purpose in Life

In the ancient world, it was common for people's names to be in-scribed on public monuments, buildings, or plaques in reward for rendering some kind of public service. This not only honored benefactors while they lived but ensured they were remembered when they died. However, if an individual subsequently did great wrong or became disgraced, one was sometimes punished by having one's name erased from all inscriptions in a phenomenon known as *damnatio memoriae*. This was seen as a terrible sanction because rather than the person and actions being remembered in the future (due to the inscriptions), they would now be forgotten. I mention this example because it illustrates one aspect of our com-mon experience that I want to reflect on: our sense of purpose.

Meaning to live for

Why would you fear *damnatio memoriae*? Or, to put it another way, why was it important to the ancients to be remembered? There are several answers to that question, but at its root there must have been a sense that their life, actions, and accomplish-ments were meaningful—literally, that they *had meaning*. The desire to be remembered presumes that there is something worth remembering, that our life *counts* in some way.

To move forward to our own lives, do we not have the same intuition? You regularly hear people saying that they want to "make a difference" in one way or another. Most of us want to feel like we are contributing to the community, or at least to some individuals within it. Often our sense of vocation or satisfaction at work comes from the belief that what we did mattered. All of this can be summed up by the claim that humans seem to require a sense of purpose in order to flourish—the feeling that we are doing something meaningful, moving towards a goal, that our contributions matter.

This can be confirmed by looking at what happens when we lack a sense of purpose in life: many who are unemployed for significant periods of time can feel depressed or insecure; without a sense of direction, we experience boredom. There are substantial links between destructive behavior (whether that be self-destructive addictions, criminality, or other-directed violence) and the sense that our lives lack purpose or that we have no place in a community in which to contribute in a meaningful way. In short, when we do not find the content of our days meaningful, we struggle; human flourishing seems to require the belief that life has purpose. How might we make sense of this common experience, not just in our culture but back through the centuries? What narrative, or worldview, can best explain our behavior—that we live as if there is purpose in life?

The logical conclusions of naturalism

This is one of the points at which naturalism seems least able to explain our experience of life. Our sense that our existence matters and that we have something to contribute can certainly be considered as an evolutionary advantage; the communal impulse of making a difference may be seen as one reason why we made it as a species in the battle for survival. But this is just to *describe* what we observe; it does not *explain* where it comes from.

More to the point, if we are simply the result of impersonal material beginnings, then the development of life is not something that has happened on purpose (because to be on purpose requires choice, which is something only possessed by people); it is not something that has goals or aims (for the same reason). Instead, it is the unguided random process of physical laws and matter. I find it impossible to see how that story can claim that life is meaningful. If we take this worldview seriously, then we must say that any sense of a purpose that extends beyond our genetic survival is illusory. This then presents us with two options: we must either face up to the illusion and accept the meaninglessness of life, or we can choose to consciously remain in the illusion and try to enjoy it—that is, to deliberately live in a fairy tale.

The first option was taken by the atheist philosopher Nietzsche who claimed that humanity had the task of creating its own meaning: we must decide our own purpose and the values we want to live by. But this approach never resolves the issue, for purpose ends up being just about me; and if meaning is something we each invent, why should you accept my view about what matters? Why should I accept yours? We end up with a million different purposes, and we still have not explained our sense that our lives are meaningful *not just for ourselves*. After all, if you make your own meaning, why should any of us remember you when you are dead? Nietzsche's story is not a happy one. He ended up going mad, which may be seen as the logical conclusion of his worldview.

The second option is one many people currently take. Although they say they accept the naturalist worldview, they do not live like it. I suggest this might be a good reason to consider whether that worldview should be rejected. After all, what integrity is there in continuing to live in a way that your beliefs cannot explain?

Other possibilities

If we were to reject naturalism, we may be tempted to a version of pantheism (that everything is God, and nothing that exists is distinct from God). Perhaps we feel that life is meaningful because we are spiritually united with the rest of the universe, waiting to experience the rapture of a deeper union with the divine everything. Again, though, I cannot see how this explains either our sense that we are meaningful as individual people or that we have a specific purposeful contribution to make. In this worldview, there is no story that could justify the feeling that my life matters in its particular history; the goal is simply to reach the end. Neither does it explain our sense that we are somehow responsible *for* the world we live in, the desire to be active, rather than passive, in making a difference in our communities and our world.

In contrast, the Christian narrative both echoes and explains our experience of life. We are indeed deeply connected with the world, but we are not dissolved into it; we do anticipate a deeper union with God but one in which our individuality is preserved and fully developed. In the Christian worldview, we are created with purpose. We have work to do and tasks to complete; we are called to play our own part in the unfolding of beauty, goodness, and love. Our choices matter. Our histories are important. We want to make a difference because we were always meant to live and work for the development of communities. We want to make a difference because the way the world is at the moment is not fully how it is designed to be, and we are called to be part of putting things right. Our sense of purpose is not an illusion but is part of what it means to be made in God's image. We do in fact have purpose. Life is meaningful, because we are created *for something*—to know and enjoy God, one another, and the material world; to take our place and fulfil our role in God's kingdom. So I am a Christian because it is this worldview that best coheres with the human experience of living as if there is purpose in life.

11

Because We Distract
Ourselves

To come to grips with the subject of this chapter, I propose a simple experiment for you to try. Would you be willing to find a place indoors where you will be undisturbed and sit there in silence for an hour, with no phone, books, other people, or activities of any kind? To have an hour with absolutely nothing other than yourself and silence? This is a very simple task, but I find that most people are not willing to do this. Why?

Compulsive distraction

We live in what is likely to be the most distracted human culture ever to have existed. Two-screening is common; we spend hours every day on our smartphones (flicking between apps, entertainment, news, various communications); our attention spans are ever shorter; and so on. This has been widely written about and is indisputable: we spend much of our lives distracted. The desire for distraction is not just a modern phenomenon, though. Blaise Pascal, writing in the seventeenth century, noted the same human tendency. He observes that we throw ourselves into various activities, but we never seem happy when we achieve what we are working for:

> When men are reproached for pursuing so eagerly something that could never satisfy them, their proper answer, if they really thought about it, ought to be that they simply want a violent and vigorous occupation to take their minds off themselves.[1]

We fill up our lives with work, activities, relationships, entertainment, hobbies, etc., with the result that we rarely ever stop for any significant length of time. When you do, I would be inclined to bet you get your phone out. Why is this? Why do we shy away from an hour on our own? Why do we cram our lives so full? What is it from which we are trying to distract ourselves?

Distracted from what?

In the above quote, Pascal claims that all our distraction is an attempt to take our minds off ourselves. I think he is right. It seems to me that most people refuse to sit silently on their own for an hour because they find what comes up in their thoughts to be uncomfortable. This may be memories or situations they find distressing or anxieties they are trying to avoid, but often it is also the big questions of life: Am I really doing the right thing? What is this all about anyway? Am I truly happy? It is as if we have many questions and issues pressing upon us for attention, and we fear that if we allow ourselves to become still, we will have to face them. Pascal writes this: "Being unable to cure death, wretchedness and ignorance, men have decided, in order to be happy, not to think about such things."[2] The example of death is a very good one. This is simply one of the unavoidable realities of human life, but many of us cannot bring ourselves to think about it for very long. It poses uncomfortable questions, like "Is there life after death?" Or, "If there is, how does that relate to the idea of God?" Or even,

1. Pascal, *Pensées*, 39.
2. Pascal, *Pensées*, 37.

"If not, is there any point to all I do while I am still alive?" As another seventeenth-century French intellectual, François de La Rochefoucauld, puts it, "Neither the sun nor death can be looked at steadily."[3]

There is perhaps a second discomfort that keeps us distracted in addition to this, which is the sense that we are in some way *accountable*. We discussed in previous chapters that we all have a sense of objective morality and of justice. By consequence, we all, I think, tend to experience an inner sense of obligation, the feeling that we *should* do this or do that. Our conscience twinges when we fail to meet such standards, and we tend to want to justify our behavior when it is condemned. These are all aspects of this experience of feeling accountable in our lives—but accountable to whom? Such a feeling goes beyond a sense of accountability to one another, because we still have these feelings when no one else is watching. Morality and justice press upon each of us individually. We find ourselves feeling accountable to these standards, which raises the haunting question of what kind of reality exists that is both the source and the power behind these standards, a question we are often disinclined to think through to its logical conclusions.

The despair of distraction

Our tendency to distract ourselves from our thoughts and questions is a desperate attempt for happiness, but to return to Pascal a final time:

> The only thing that consoles us for our miseries is diversion. And yet it is the greatest of our miseries. For it is that above all which prevents us thinking about ourselves and leads us imperceptibly to destruction. But that we should be bored, and boredom would drive us to seek

3. François de La Rochefoucauld, *Collected Maxims and Other Reflections*, translated by E. H. Blackmore et al. (Oxford, UK: Oxford University Press, 2007), 11.

some more solid means of escape, but diversion passes
our time and brings us imperceptibly to death.[4]

To keep running from what disturbs us is, in the end, to confirm
our unhappiness. C. S. Lewis, who wrote about similar themes in
his *Mere Christianity*, says this:

> Comfort is the one thing you cannot get by looking for
> it. If you look for the truth, you may find comfort in
> the end: if you look for comfort you will not get either
> comfort or truth—only soft soap and wishful thinking to
> begin with and, in the end, despair.[5]

It seems to me that in order to make sense of what we have
discussed in this chapter, we need to say two things. First, each of
us has some inkling that we were made for happiness, for joy, for
rest; our unhappiness is largely due to the feeling that *it was not
meant to be like this*, that we were made for more. That is why we
avoid our miseries. On some level, we know life should not be this
way, but we do not know how to fix it. Second, we must say that
something has therefore gone badly wrong. We are not the people
we feel we should be, and we cannot find the happiness we know
we were made for. We are accountable, but we fail to live up to the
standards we feel are right. If this were not true, we would probably find it easier to sit in a room and be undistracted . . .

If we want to make sense of life, our worldview needs to be
able to explain our addiction to distraction and the despair it ultimately delivers. I am a Christian because that is exactly the narrative that Christianity tells—that we were made for greatness but
that we have gone wrong. We have chosen to rule our own lives and
therefore find them unmanageable. We are indeed accountable,
and we should feel uncomfortable at our failure to live up to such
standards. All we have discussed in this chapter is exactly what
we should expect, if Christianity is true. Of course, the Christian
worldview also tells of the way out of our misery—the possibility

4. Pascal, *Pensées*, 120.
5. C. S. Lewis, *The Complete C. S. Lewis Signature Classics* (New York:
HarperCollins, 2002), 36.

of forgiveness, reconciliation, healing, purpose, and peace—but that is to be found in other books. The point here is that our compulsive distraction demands an explanation that Christianity is well able to provide.

SECTION 2.1

EXAMINING HISTORY

The Resurrection

12

BECAUSE OF THE EVIDENCE THAT JESUS LIVED AND DIED

C hristians believe that a man called Jesus died by crucifixion.
Crosses can often be found on church walls, and many de-
pictions of Jesus have him on the cross. Of course, Christianity
claims much more than that (indeed, its most outrageous claim
is that Jesus not only died but came back to life again), but it does
not claim less. This is obviously an important issue, because if
Jesus never lived (and died), Christianity is both a lie and a waste
of time. The evidence that he did is part of why I consider my
Christian faith to be reasonable.

Historical method

Any historian who wants to work out what happened in the past
faces some challenges. The main one is that we were not there! We
have no firsthand knowledge of what occurred, and so we have to
rely on historical sources, primarily the writings of other people.
These never give us the complete picture or answer all the questions we may have; sometimes they are contradictory or difficult
to understand. The job of the historian is to put the pieces together
to work out what happened, or rather what seems the *most likely*

thing to have happened, that can explain our evidence. The job is even harder without photographs and videos (although even these are not always reliable), so to go back two thousand years and work out what happened in the ancient world is a tricky business. Historians have developed methods to try to help them work out if something really happened or not. For example:

1. If there are lots of sources for an event, it is more likely to have happened, especially when these sources come from different people or are independent of one another.

2. Evidence that comes from soon after the time of the event it is describing is, on the whole, more reliable, as is evidence from people who were themselves there (as opposed to others who just heard about the event).

That all may seem obvious, but it is important to keep in mind that any historical claim must use principles like these. It is also worth remembering that our historical sources were written by *people*—which allows us to develop other principles as well:

3. When we do have a lot of evidence, we can usually work out which sources seem more reliable; some ancient writers were more truthful and accurate than others.

4. We all tend to record history—either a narrative of the past or simply the events we experience and observe—in line with our own biases, interests, and agendas (as in the quip "history is written by the winners"). So when an ancient author reports something that portrays him (or his interests) in a bad light, we can usually expect this to be trustworthy.

Taking this on board, what is our evidence that Jesus lived and died?

Christian sources

Our best sources are four accounts of Jesus's life written by different people in the first century AD. The accounts are now known as Matthew, Mark, Luke, and John (known collectively as the Gospels) and later became part of the Bible. All four describe Jesus's life and teaching, his interactions with other people, his actions, and his death. Although they share some sources, each of them also presents unique historical material. Despite having a variety of interests and styles, all four tell the same basic story, appear to be historically and geographically accurate where we can test them, and agree on the major points. Mark was probably the earliest, but all were written before the eyewitnesses to Jesus's life had died; in fact, they were all written by, or relied on, these eyewitnesses. The Gospels have been incredibly well preserved since they were written and, by normal historical standards, present strong evidence for Jesus's existence and his death.

The Gospels stand up well on principles 1–3, then, but it is worth briefly commenting on the fourth as well. If you read the Gospels, one of the interesting things is how badly those who provided much of the source material for the accounts (the first followers of Jesus) come off. They regularly make mistakes and fail; at times, they seem weak, petty, or cowardly; they often let Jesus down, even abandoning him at his death. This is not the story you would tell if you were making it up. Perhaps most notable is that in all our accounts, Jesus's death is by crucifixion, a particular *kind* of death in the first century. The Jews saw it as a death for those who had been cursed by God, and the Romans considered it a particularly shameful (and painful) way to die, reserved for the worst kind of criminals or slaves. In that culture, it was absurd to claim that a man who had been crucified was worthy of admiration, emulation, and worship. And yet that was what was claimed. If we refer back to our fourth principle, these observations should increase our confidence in the reliability of these accounts.

Non-Christian sources

The Gospels are not the only evidence we have from Christian sources. We might also mention the letters of Paul, for example, Paul having been an early Christian leader who had personal contact with Jesus's family and recorded this in his letters. However, if this were all our evidence, we might still be suspicious. "Perhaps all this was written to perpetuate the religious myth that they were a part of," we might think. "They cannot be trusted because they are not neutral." My view is that they would still stand up relatively well as reliable historical sources even if they were the only ones we had (after all, there was no big church or religious institution to justify back then, just a ragtag bunch of Christians in insignificant groups across a small part of the Roman Empire). We do not have to argue that one out, though, because there are other non-Christian sources that give us evidence for Jesus and his death:

- The Roman historian Tacitus, writing in the early second century AD, was hostile to both Jews and Christians, but he mentions Jesus and that he was crucified, dating the event and mentioning the Roman official responsible, both details in agreement with the gospel accounts.

- The Jewish historian Josephus, writing towards the end of the first century AD, does the same, confirming Jesus, his death, its date and the responsible Roman officer. In a separate passage he mentions Jesus and that he had a brother. Another Jewish source for Jesus and his death is the Talmud, although this evidence comes from a much later period.

- The Greek philosopher Celses wrote a large book criticising Christianity. Although he attacks many aspects of Christian belief and practice, he never contests the existence of Jesus.

- Finally, the witty author Lucian of Samosata, who wrote in the second century AD, also wrote of Jesus and his death. Lucian was particularly unsympathetic to Christians, considering them to be both stupid and immoral.

It is worth finishing this chapter by saying that I am not aware of any serious historian who thinks Jesus was not a real man who died in Jerusalem at the hands of the Romans. The historical evidence is compelling. To have so many sources of good reliability, from different perspectives, in agreement on the main points, is remarkable. It is far more substantial than the evidence for many other historical facts we take for granted. So, I consider Christianity reasonable because of the historical evidence for Jesus's life and death.

13

Because of the Evidence That Jesus Rose from the Dead

I suggested in the last chapter that the evidence that Jesus lived and died is compelling. But if that was all the evidence indicated, then this would be historically interesting, perhaps, but unimportant for me and you today. The claim that Jesus rose from the dead, by contrast, has significant implications for all of us, if it is true. This is the central claim of the Christian faith: namely, that Jesus was a real person who lived, died, and *came back to life again in history*. Whether or not this belief is reasonable is the focus of this chapter.

Clarifying our options

Before we look at the evidence, I want to make a couple of observations about what we should expect. One of two things happened:

1. Jesus rose from the dead.
2. Jesus did not rise from the dead.

These are the only options. Similarly, there are only three conclusions any human may come to when considering the claim that Jesus rose from the dead:

    a. Jesus rose from the dead.

    b. Jesus did not rise from the dead.

    c. I do not know whether he rose from the dead or not.

Now, let us use our imagination for a moment. If Jesus did actually rise from the dead (option 1) and if somebody was an eyewitness of this event (somebody actually saw Jesus risen from the dead), then that person may well conclude that Jesus did, in fact, rise from the dead (option *a*). In such a scenario, this person is probably going to become a Christian and join one of the first churches. One thing we should expect, then, is that any evidence for the resurrection will come from Christian sources. It is quite possible for someone to believe Jesus lived and died without becoming a Christian (like Josephus, Tacitus, Celsus, and Lucian in the last chapter); it is less easy to believe that Jesus rose from the dead without becoming one.

Now imagine that Jesus did not rise from the dead (option 2). If this is the case, then no one saw Jesus alive again. Any people who claimed they did were lying or mistaken. In this scenario, we would expect humans to conclude option *b* (because that would be true and there would be no reliable evidence to the contrary) or option *c*. In this scenario, the challenge is to explain why some concluded option *a*.

Finally, as we discussed in the introduction to this book, it is not possible to present absolute proof for conclusions *a*, *b*, or *c*. There is no undoubtable evidence or anything of the sort. Rather, what we are looking for is what is the most *reasonable* belief. So then, what is the evidence for the resurrection?

Evidence

The first kind of evidence is the testimony of people who claimed to have met Jesus after he had died. Some of these stories are captured in the Gospels, others we know about from the letters and writings of the first Christians. What is interesting is that these resurrection appearances do not seem to be like most other religious visions; the accounts go out of their way to describe how physically real Jesus appeared to be. They not only saw him, but they touched him. He spoke to people and answered their questions. He ate with them. He went a whole day's journey with two of them, talking on the road. He appeared to individuals, small groups, and large groups. He appeared during a specific period (around forty days after his death) and then did not appear anymore, with one exception. There is no psychological explanation that can easily account for this as a series of visionary appearances brought on by trauma or grief. There are simply too many people in too wide a variety of situations, with a complex mix of similarity (they all said it was Jesus) and difference (in the type and content of experience). In summary, part of the evidence for the resurrection is the testimony of those who encountered Jesus alive again after his death.

The second piece of evidence is that Jesus's body disappeared after his death and burial. There is no doubt that Jesus really died. The Romans who killed him were professional executioners whose own lives would be taken if he survived. Before they took him down from the cross, they stabbed a spear into his side, where the flow of blood and water medically verified his death. He was then taken and buried in a tomb, sealed by a large stone, and guarded by Roman soldiers. His followers did not expect him to rise from the dead; they went home in grief. And yet a couple of days later, when they went to tend to his body, as was normal Jewish practice, the tomb was empty. This could be the case only if Jesus had risen from the dead or somebody had taken the body.

The Roman authorities had no reason to take the body. In fact, they had a very good reason not to: interfering with dead bodies would have risked offending the Jews. Jerusalem was crowded because Jesus died in the middle of a Jewish festival and the crowds were already volatile and hostile. The individual soldiers would not have taken the body, for they would have been punished for failing in their duties. The Jews who wanted Jesus dead cannot have taken the body, for if they had, they would have surely produced it when the first Christians claimed Jesus had risen from the dead. So who does that leave? It has occasionally been suggested that the first Christians stole the body and then constructed a lie that Jesus had risen from the dead. Is this plausible?

The next chapter is all about the behavior of Jesus's followers and family, so we'll have more to say then. For now, I want to observe that if Jesus's followers were lying and trying to persuade people Jesus had risen from the dead, then they went about it in a very odd way. For a start, their written accounts of Jesus's resurrection agree that the first eyewitness were women; but back then, women were considered unreliable (for example, their testimony in court was worth less than that of men). Why not invent a story with more credible witnesses? Furthermore, they admit that some of them doubted that Jesus had come back to life, which seems out of place if you are telling a story that had been made up to convince people of his resurrection. These are just two examples of many details that are very hard to make sense of if the disciples stole the body. In truth, the Gospels simply do not read as literature designed to convince people of an invented claim. They are much better understood as an account of, and an attempt to make sense of, the disciples' experience of Jesus. In summary, there are no convincing candidates for the removal of Jesus's body.

We must not forget that our ancient sources come from humans whose behavior and choices we can seek to make sense of. When we remember this and treat our sources accordingly, we can ask what the most reasonable explanation of the evidence is. I am a Christian because I find the evidence of the empty tomb and resurrection appearances most reasonably explained by the claim that Jesus did, in fact, rise from the dead.

14

BECAUSE OF THE BEHAVIOR
OF HIS FRIENDS AND FAMILY

When we discuss the resurrection, it is possible to forget
that it was real people who knew Jesus, spent time with
him, followed him, wrote about him, and formed the first church.
Rather than thinking of them as normal human beings, we can
end up talking about them as if they were two-dimensional char-
acters or idiots. This is a shame, as this can often lead us to unre-
alistic conclusions. If we want to arrive at reasonable beliefs about
Jesus and the resurrection, we will want to consider how we might
explain the behavior of those *people* who were closest to him.

Prepared to die

For a start, I want to think a bit more about a possibility we described in the last chapter—that Jesus's first followers made up the
story of his resurrection, claiming something they knew to be a
lie. This is the kind of argument that gets thrown around the table
down the pub, but I have always found this unconvincing, for the
simple reason that some of the first Christians (those who would
have made up the story) were killed because of what they claimed.
Crucifixion is one of the most painful methods of execution we

have ever invented; is it plausible that Peter (one of Jesus's disciples who became a leader in the first church), for example, would willingly have been crucified for something he knew was a lie? And Peter was not the first. His cousin James had already been killed, amongst others. People will die for something about which they are mistaken, but I do not think it likely that they will die for the sake of something they know to be a lie. So it seems to me that the theory that the disciples made up Jesus's resurrection is implausible. They devoted their lives to telling others about Jesus and were prepared to die for their claims.

An unexpected resurrection

We should also remember that the accounts of Jesus's life are all agreed that when he died, his disciples did not expect him to come back to life again. They went home in grief, thinking it was all over. It is not the case that they expected Jesus to rise from the dead and were determined to make it real if it did not happen. There was no such expectation. Instead, our sources indicate that when Jesus had tried to talk about rising from the dead, they had not understood him (which is not much of a surprise, given they were normal people; what would you think if one of the sanest people you had ever met began talking about coming back from the dead?). It was only after the event that they understood, in retrospect, what he had been trying to tell them. All this is to say that if they *had* decided to make up Jesus's resurrection, it would have been an impulse out of the blue that Jesus's first followers would simultaneously all have bought into. I find this entirely implausible.

Family dynamics

Another interesting group is Jesus's family. The Gospels tell us that while Jesus was alive and teaching his followers, his family were not supportive. On at least one occasion, they tried to convince him to come back home and stop teaching what they thought was, at best, mistaken—at worst, immoral. His mother and brothers (his father Joseph seems to have died before Jesus began teaching in public) were not convinced by his claims to be the Messiah and did not join his group of followers. And then, less than ten years after his death, his brothers were leaders in the early church; they were writing letters to churches, presiding over critical meetings, and considered important figures by others. What happened? When your brother dies for teaching a message with which you disagreed, what would persuade you to change your mind (in his absence), suddenly believe he had risen from the dead, and risk your life by becoming part of the movement he started (that you were unwilling to join while he was alive and no one had yet died)? We all know what family can be like. To swallow your pride, admit your brother was right, and then risk your reputation (and possibly your life) by joining the church is quite a turnaround. The only clue we have is in one of the letters written by Paul, where he notes that Jesus appeared to his brothers when he had risen from the dead. This would be a sufficient reason to make sense of their change of direction. If Jesus did not persuade them while he was alive, the most plausible reason they would become radical followers of his movement is that they too truly believed he had risen from the dead.

Paul

And then there is Paul himself. Paul was a zealous Jew, who passionately believed that the early church was a problem that needed to be stamped out. Not only was it a political threat to the Jewish nation, but for Paul, this was a heresy that must not be allowed to continue. He had Christians killed (the most famous being Stephen), and he went from city to city searching out the church and destroying it. He was as hostile towards the church as anyone about whom we know. And yet we find that at some point in his life, he started preaching the Christian message, debating with the Jews with whom he was previously in agreement, travelling across the Roman empire founding churches, and embracing a huge amount of suffering to do so. He, too, chose to die for his Christian faith. Once again, we must look for a plausible explanation. It is not as if Paul was failing when he was persecuting the church, for the churches were in fear of him. He had no close friends or family who were Christians; it was not personally or politically expedient for him to become one. In fact, to become a Christian entailed a much harder life than the one he had. Again, it seems to me the most reasonable explanation is the one that Paul himself gave—that he, too, met the risen Jesus and had an experience that changed everything. From that time on, he was a different man.

Normal people

In the next section, we will go on to talk about the rise of the church, but for now, I hope to have indicated some of the people involved whose behavior demands an explanation. As we think which explanation is most reasonable, we must remember that they were humans like us. They were his brothers who grew up with him, his friends who accompanied him for many years, his enemies who hated him. When we take this seriously, the evidence that he really did rise from the dead becomes even more weighty. I have not found a more reasonable explanation that can account for the degree of change in that many people all at the same time, to choose a life that was much harder and led several of them to their deaths.

I am a Christian because the behavior of the people dealt with in this chapter can best be explained if those people were convinced that Jesus really did rise from the dead; and the most reasonable explanation for why they held this belief is that he did, in fact, rise from the dead.

SECTION 2.2

EXAMINING HISTORY

The Church

15

BECAUSE OF THE EXISTENCE
AND GROWTH OF THE CHURCH

When we are considering our beliefs and working out a reasonable worldview, we can tend to do this in a very individualistic way. This is no surprise, as we live in a culture that tells us that it is our personal experience, opinions, and thoughts that matter most—and this is fine, to an extent. As is obvious in this book so far, I think that we need to take personal responsibility for evaluating and changing, if necessary, our beliefs; but our individualistic bent can lead us to miss important evidence that is more corporate in nature. In short, beliefs are held by (and shape) not only individuals but also communities, and it is appropriate to ask what this corporate dimension might add to the picture. These next three chapters explore this idea, for I consider it reasonable to be a Christian partly because of the community of the church through the centuries.

The unlikely existence and survival of the early church

It is remarkable that the first church even survived. Jesus was a divisive figure who ruffled enough feathers of the powerful to be crucified. The first church not only continued to teach about Jesus and his worldview but proclaimed that he had risen from the dead and continued to claim (as Jesus himself did) that he was the Son of God. The two groups that held power at the time were the Romans and, to a more limited degree, the Jews. Now, to the Jews, the claims of the first church were scandalous for a few reasons: 1) the Jews were zealous monotheists, and the claim that Jesus, a human, was divine ("making him equal with God") was outrageous; 2) they considered that anyone who was crucified had been cursed by God; 3) the idea of a human being resurrected before the final judgment (that is, the end of human history as we know it) was entirely outside their current worldview. So the message of the early church inevitably disturbed many Jews and led to them persecute the first churches, killing Christians and trying to stamp out this heretical Jewish sect. (In passing, we should note again as we saw earlier how unlikely it was that any Jew would have made up such claims; they were radically controversial.)

To the Romans, the message was equally ridiculous. Influenced by Greek philosophy, the Romans would have found it very difficult to accept the idea that any kind of god would become a human being or that a human would be resurrected. Moreover, the first churches claimed that Jesus was the Son of God, was Lord, and was the only suitable object of worship, which cut against the polytheism of the Greco-Roman world and the dominance of the emperor (who was also known as "Lord" and "son of God"). So, Christians were also persecuted by Romans who could easily see their teaching as politically disruptive. The early church leader Paul said that the Christian message was "a stumbling block to the Jews and folly to the gentiles [non-Jews]."[1] He was right. If we add to this that the first churches had no particularly powerful advocates and that they lived in a region that was, politically, highly charged, we might wonder how on earth a community with no political or social power, teaching such an offensive and implausible message, doubly persecuted, even managed to survive.

1. This is from the Bible in the book called First Corinthians, chapter 1, verse 23.

The growth of the church before Constantine

But it did survive. Not much more than three hundred years later, around half the Roman Empire had converted to Christianity. The historian Rodney Stark has worked out a plausible model that gives a growth rate of 3.4% per year.[2] If he is anywhere near the mark (and we have limited evidence with which to work), this shows that Christianity was small and fragile for quite a long time before it eventually began to blossom across the empire. Such growth was by no means inevitable. In addition to what we have already discussed, we should note that there were many other religious options for your average inhabitant of the Roman Empire: congregations gathered to worship Cybele, Bacchus, or Isis, for example. Isis is a particularly good point of comparison, as this was also an Eastern import claiming to give dynamic religious experiences and to offer benefits after death. As well as outgrowing all other options, the church was notable for encompassing broad sections of society. It was certainly growth from below (after all, Constantine aligned the empire with Christianity only after more than half his subjects had converted), but that is not to say it was only growth amongst the low (the poor, the disempowered, slaves, etc.). In fact, the church grew significantly amongst those with socioeconomic means as well, certainly after the first century CE and possibly before.

The growth of the church ever since

We tend to think of Christianity as a Western religion, but over the first six hundred years, the church grew through the Latin West, the Greek East, North Africa, and across the Middle East. The latter two were decimated by the rise of Islam, but these were the original pillars of the church. Now, Christianity has spread all over the globe to be the largest global religion and possibly the fastest growing (it is neck and neck with Islam). Importantly, this means that Christianity has spread across all kinds of cultures and

2. Stark, *Triumph of Christianity*, 153–65.

cultural differences. Many religions or worldviews remain tied to a particular culture or political system, but not Christianity. (Christianity may, over time, tend to produce a particular kind of culture or politics, but that is a different matter.) Moreover, this global spread has been despite intense persecution, a situation that is still ongoing in many countries today.

We might summarize by saying that the odds of survival were stacked against the first church, but that church flourished despite competition and persecution to become dominant across the four regions I identified earlier. From there, it has crossed every significant cultural barrier to become, despite significant persecution, the biggest religion in the world and continues to grow. What might this have to say to our consideration of the reasonableness of the Christian worldview?

What no one should claim is that apparent success shows that Christianity (or any other worldview) is true. Many widely held beliefs turn out to be false. Nor is it the case that all those reporting to be Christians are following Jesus in any substantial way; no doubt, for many, it is simply an inherited cultural identity. However, the survival and growth of the church should give us pause for thought. First, if the survival of the church is so unlikely, it may be reasonable for Christians to think that God may have been involved in some way. Second, if so many people, in such a variety of cultures, across two millennia of history, have found the claims of Christianity compelling, then we may at least want to examine them seriously for ourselves.

16

BECAUSE OF THE NATURE
AND ACTIONS OF THE CHURCH

In this chapter I suggest that one of the reasons we can consider Christianity to be reasonable is because of the historical track record of the actions of the church. This might seem an odd argument to try to make, for, after all, does not religion cause wars? Have not hundreds of thousands of people died fighting because of Christianity? In recent decades, the rise of fundamentalism in Islam and Christianity seems to have fuelled global violence and terrorism. If we look through history, can we not find many moral horrors that have been justified on the grounds of religious faith? Is this not all good cause to doubt religious worldviews?

Or so the story often goes. I do not doubt that there are many evils that have been done under the banner of Christianity, but a sober look at history tells us a lot more than that. In truth, any worldview or ideology can be misappropriated—secular or religious—and all worldviews have so been. There is no innocent lineage, no set of beliefs that has never been used to justify violence. Unfortunately, humans will, at times, grasp at anything to justify their violence, desire for power, and so on (which of course needs explaining, when we all have such a strong sense of morality and justice, as we discussed in previous chapters). What we cannot do, then, is say "Well, there is a black mark here, so this worldview must be thrown out," for we would have nothing left to believe. Rather, I suggest we must do two things:

First, we must look at the claims of each worldview and assess whether, in principle, this set of beliefs can justify our desire for and lead to things like human flourishing, ordered society, peace, moral goodness, etc. A worldview that cannot do this is less plausible than one that can, given that we all desire these ends.

Second, we must look at the overall track record of each worldview lived out over long periods of time, taking the big picture into account and evaluating actions in their historical context. A worldview that fairly consistently (if imperfectly) lives in line with its stated beliefs will be more plausible than one that does not.

In previous chapters I have already discussed why I think that the Christian worldview provides better grounds for the kind of desires I have listed in the first point; this chapter will focus on the second.

The place of love in Christianity

When Jesus was asked about what was most important in the kind of life humans should live, he replied that we were to love God with our hearts, minds, souls, and strength and to love others as ourselves. He put love at the center of what it means to be human. One of the earliest Christian letters says that he then showed us what he meant by love when he chose to be crucified for the sake of others. In consequence, there are two important points we should note.

First, this kind of love—what we used to mean by the word *charity*—was not a moral virtue in the Greco-Roman world in which Christianity developed. To give to those who were poor or to serve those weaker than you was not a desirable characteristic but a sign of weakness or faulty character. But Jesus placed other-directed love at the center of his church. If today we all tend to see this as commonsense morality, we owe it to the fact that our culture has been deeply shaped by Christianity.

Second, given the worldview of Christianity, we should expect the church to be at the forefront of working out how best to love others holistically: through charity, education, practical care, developing systems of justice, building society, protecting the vulnerable, working for peace—in short, to pursue the fullest human flourishing. Of course, for Christians, love will include telling others about Jesus and his way of life, as they believe this to be central to human flourishing, but there is no antithesis between this and everything else. As Jesus made clear: for the Christian, loving God and loving others come together.

The actions of the church

Although the failures of the church to live up to its calling are regularly rehearsed, there is a long history of meaningful and substantial actions that, though always imperfect, demand our attention. I will list a selection in what remains of this chapter.

In its earliest centuries, the church chose to treat women differently from the prevailing culture. They rejected the usual practice of exposing unwanted children (usually girls) to death, arguing that all life was valuable. They also refused abortions (which were extremely dangerous to women) and rejected the Roman norm of making girls marry young (the age of twelve or thirteen was not unusual at the time; but Christian women tended to marry in their later teenage years). The moral principle of seeing each human life as valuable also underwrote the Christian-led opposition to the slave trade in eighteenth-century Britain and to various racial justice movements in the twentieth century. It is also the driving principle between church-led forgiveness and reconciliation work currently going on in South Africa and Northern Ireland.

Again, right from the beginning, the church was noted for its care for the poor, notably the most vulnerable in society, like prisoners and widows. This grew to the extent that in the fourth century, the Roman Emperor Julian, frustrated by the growth of Christianity, wrote that "the impious Galileans [Christians] support not only their own poor but ours as well."[1] In eighteenth-century England, John Howard and Elizabeth Fry led far-reaching prison reforms; in the nineteenth century, George Müller established orphanages and schools for the poor. Today, many of the organizations that have pioneered attempts to relieve global poverty are Christian, and missionaries regularly seek to relieve hardship and meet local needs.

Education has also been a means by which the church has sought to love others, whether that be in monasteries that sought to preserve culture and learning through times of societal breakdown or the establishing of schools and universities throughout Europe in the Middle Ages (all the oldest universities were founded by the church). We have already discussed how it was the culture of Christian Europe that enabled the development of modern science, and it was the attempt of the Church of England to establish schools in every parish that was the foundation for developing the (now widely accepted) principle of free education for all children.

These are only a few examples among many that could be given. The aim is not to claim the church has never done harm; evidently it has (and, in fact, the Christian worldview includes an understanding of sin that would lead us to expect that this will sometimes be the case). However, we can say that Christianity is primarily responsible for the development of charity (other-directed love) as a moral virtue,[2] and, when we take a broad view of history, there is much to show the church acting in line with its beliefs, including the ability to be self-critical and to keep reforming and changing. I am not convinced that the community of any other worldview comes out better under proper comparison, which is why this is one of the reasons that I am a Christian.

1. He wrote this in a letter to a Roman (pagan) priest. The translation I have used is taken from the three-volume *The Works of the Emperor Julian*, translated by W. C. Wright, in the Loeb Classical Library (1913–1923). It can be found at 22.430D in the collection of Julian's letters.

2. This is argued at length by David Bentley Hart in his book *Atheist Delusions* (New Haven, CT: Yale University Press, 2009).

17

BECAUSE OF THE INTELLECTUAL HERITAGE OF THE CHURCH

W hat we call water consists of molecules that have one oxygen atom bonded with two hydrogen atoms. I imagine you already know this. Do you believe this because you have personally investigated and categorized different elements? Or because you carried out detailed scientific experiments on water? I imagine, like me, that you know this because you learned it from other people. Of course, we have been given reasonable explanations, and the experiments done by others are, in theory, repeatable, so we *could* do them if we wanted to. But most of us know that water is H_2O because this knowledge has been passed on to us. So much of what we know is like this. None of us stands alone; we all stand within a heritage or, perhaps better put, within a tradition.

This is not only inevitable but desirable. Imagine if you had to establish everything yourself without relying on anyone else's knowledge. You would barely be able to know anything (for example, the existence of any part of the country you had not personally visited). We rely on the testimony of other humans all the time, and this is to be welcomed. Furthermore, living within a heritage of knowledge does not prevent us being critical, for we often overturn "knowledge" of the past on the basis of new discoveries or ideas. We might say that the tradition passed on to us is what allows us to make progress in our own time, which will sometimes involve rethinking or rejecting what has been given to us. Hopefully, you can see that this is a description of every one of our lives; we all stand within a tradition.

Evaluating traditions

This is one way to think about worldviews: they are traditions that are handed on to us, within which we stand (consciously or unconsciously). When we are weighing up how reasonable a worldview is, it makes sense, therefore, to analyze its heritage. Who has contributed to this tradition? How might we assess them? To what extent is this tradition self-aware and self-critical? To what extent has it tried to deal with the difficult questions that face all worldviews? This is not a simple tick-box exercise that will give us an automatic rating of how good a worldview is, but it seems reasonable to me to give more credence to worldviews that have been held and developed by a significant number of thoughtful people, whose work stands up well to critical examination, who are aware of and have addressed points of difficulty, and who have been self-critical of the tradition in which they stand.

The Christian intellectual heritage

In previous chapters, we have already touched on the historical commitment of the church to education: establishing schools and universities, preserving learning in monasteries (and other church institutions), providing the impetus for the development of modern science, or championing the education of common people. The main purpose of this chapter is to sketch the strength of the intellectual tradition within the church that has been passed down through the centuries.

We might start by noting some of the Christians who are widely held to be amongst the most brilliant thinkers of the last two millennia. I have quoted Blaise Pascal a number of times through this book, but other well-known figures include Augustine, Thomas Aquinas, Isaac Newton, Johannes Kepler, Descartes, Martin Luther, J. S. Bach, Immanuel Kant, Friedrich Schleiermacher, and Jonathan Edwards. This is an intimidating list (and we could add many more names), but the point is not only that there have been some clever people amongst the ranks of the church but that they have consistently turned their minds to the analysis, critique, and development of the Christian worldview.

One important and recurrent feature of this process has been the willingness of Christianity to incorporate truth into its worldview that comes from a variety of sources. Initially, of course, Christianity grew from the roots of Judaism and is itself accurately seen as a continuation of the Jewish tradition, before Judaism itself became quite different in the first few centuries AD. In the same period of time, Christianity recognized and integrated the Greek philosophical tradition, of which Plato's writings proved to be the most influential. In the Middle Ages, the rediscovery of the works of Aristotle also led to the critical integration of Aristotle's achievements into Christian theology and philosophy.

This ability to learn from and integrate truth from many sources demonstrates, in part, the self-awareness and self-critical ability of Christianity over time. Many of the thinkers I have listed had significant disagreements with one another. Some of them espoused relatively unusual beliefs (Kant's Christianity, for example, was quite unorthodox). This should show us that the Christian intellectual heritage is not one big echo chamber or a succession of unthinking agreement. On the contrary, it has been extremely demanding, constantly reforming, and robustly critical.

Given this, it is also important to note one other feature of this tradition, which is that, in addition to all that I have just said, it is also true that the Christian worldview has shown remarkable consistency over time, amidst all the refinement and challenge of the centuries. The Christian church still holds to the same set of fundamental beliefs now that were articulated in the first century of the existence of the church and later captured in the statements of faith that we call the creeds. None of these core beliefs has been unchallenged, but through the process of the development of Christianity, they have been repeatedly reaffirmed. This combination of core consistency and constant development also applies to the way Christians have understood the nature and place of the Bible in their worldview.

What might we conclude from all this? Perhaps it should give us pause for thought when we next hear someone talk as if Christians must be stupid for holding such obviously silly beliefs that anyone with common sense would quickly reject. I can only assume that such accusations come from ignorance. Similarly, whenever Christianity is summed up in simplistic terms, we might ask whether that kind of caricature is more a reflection of our shallow and intellectually lazy culture rather than anything that resembles the Christian heritage as it really is. Any serious investigation quickly discovers that the Christian worldview stands within a tradition of the highest intellectual caliber; we might want to ask how other worldviews fare in comparison.

Finally, one may be tempted to think that its development over time is an indication of weakness, for if it is true (and if truth is objective), then surely it should remain unchanging? I disagree. If the core claims of the Christian worldview are true (that there is an infinite God who stands behind all that exists, who can be known and invites us into his infinite beauty and love, who has created our world and called us to make sense of it), then I think we should expect the Christian worldview to remain fairly consistent in its central beliefs, whilst always developing in its details, for we will never finish the journey of discovery. If any worldview remains completely unchanged over two thousand years, we may wonder whether those who hold it are able to be self-critical or willing to learn.

So, in summary, I am a Christian partly because of the integrity, longevity, depth, consistency, dynamism, and robust intellectual weight of the heritage of the church.

SECTION 3.1

EXAMINING EXPERIENCE

Experiencing God

18

Because I Have
Experienced God

M any people claim to have experienced God. I am one of
them. It is one of the reasons I consider it reasonable to
be a Christian. Whether or not we should give weight to such a
claim depends on how we regard experience: is experience a good
guide to what is real, true, beautiful, and good, or is it thoroughly
unreliable?

The weight of experience

I would suggest that we all consistently give high regard to the reliability of our experiences; after all, having touched the hot kettle
once, we tend not to do it again. Imagine if I tried to convince you
that hearing the waves of the sea was unpleasant or that pigeons
live only in Spain. You are likely to reject my claims because you
know that these statements are false; but *how* do you know? Well,
primarily, you know because you have experienced the opposite
to be the case. Or to take another example, if you are in a loving
and faithful marriage, or you have had a reliable friend for many
years, what would you say if someone claimed that the spouse or
the friend was a cruel and malicious person, or claimed the person

you loved did not exist? We would probably find such claims impossible to believe because we *know* the person concerned. And this knowledge is based on our experience.

Of course, it is true that our experiences can be manipulated or that we can be mistaken. Television magicians have proved that it is possible to generate experiences that seem genuine but are deceitful. Similarly, we know that some experiences can be delusional. But in all such examples, the point is that they happen under *extra*ordinary circumstances (whether mental ill-health, under the influence of substances, suffering various depravations, trauma, or being subject to the psychological manipulation of others) rather than happening to ordinary people in everyday life. When we question the value of experience as a guide to reality, it is usually because one of these factors is present.

Experiencing God

We may suspect our own experience of God if it happens in such circumstances, and some seemingly religious experiences may well be caused by these factors. But my experience of God is generally quite different: it is an experience that happens in a regular, ordinary way. Experiencing God is hard to describe, but that does not mean it is particularly spectacular most of the time. It involves things like a sense of being loved, held, or cared for; the sense of being spoken to in various quite mundane ways; the intervention of God in the practical details of my life to care for me, challenge me, or otherwise communicate with me; the sense of being changed from the inside out; the sense of being given inner resources to live the kind of life about which Jesus taught; the growth of hope and love for beauty. Such experience rarely comes in hyped-up environments, when I am under physical or emotional strain or when I am in unusual circumstances, but most often occurs at normal times in normal days of my very normal life.

Explaining experience

Given that I think I experience this, there are only a few logical choices to explain my experience. Either:

1. I am not really experiencing these things.
2. My experiences are real, but my interpretation (that these are experiences of God) is false.
3. My experience of God is one factor that renders my belief in God reasonable.

Let us take each of these in turn. If I were to conclude that I was not really having these experiences (1), then I would be acting in contrast to the way I usually live. When I seem to be experiencing something, I tend to believe I *am actually* experiencing it. To conclude that I am *not really* having this experience would be logical only if there were extraordinary circumstances. The same reasoning applies to my experience of God. To try to convince myself that the experience is not really happening, despite its repeated occurrence in normal life over time, is highly irrational.

If my experiences are real, then, might they be caused by something other than God? Clearly, this is logically possible, so what we are after is not the answer that can be proved *absolutely* but the most reasonable explanation for my experience. Again, it may be helpful to clarify the options. If my experience is real, what could we consider that may explain my experience:

a. God (which I believe to be the case)
b. Myself
c. Other people
d. Other non-human spiritual beings
e. Other environmental factors

How plausible are these alternatives? It is unlikely to be *c*, as many times I experience God, I am alone. This is not to say that my experience is untouched by the influence of others; I have learned much about prayer, for example, from those who have gone before me. In this sense, my experience is shaped by others, but this is a far cry from saying that my experience can be fully *explained* by the influence of others. A guide may be able to show me the path through the mountains, but he cannot create the mountains themselves. Finally, on this point, there are occasions where people do seem to exercise control over the experience of others (like the magicians referenced earlier, or perhaps an intense cult), but this kind of manipulation is the exception, not the norm. When coming to terms with experiencing God, we have to explain the norm.

Option *b* is most likely to be claimed by those who would argue religious experience is caused by certain brain functions, meditative techniques, or psychological wish-fulfilment. It may be the case that my brain is capable of giving me such experiences under the right conditions, but I doubt whether this is plausible, given the kind of experience of God I describe. It is one thing to suggest that my wish-fulfilment can give me an experience of a father-figure, or that my meditation can give me a sense of peace; it is another thing to suggest that such factors can organize unexpected gifts of money at the exact time I have unpredicted financial needs, enable me to love my enemies, or explain the experience of having my plans overturned and rearranged in my experiences of God. In fact, so many times, experiencing God is distinctly *not* like experiencing an aspect of myself but experiencing an other. If *b* were true, then I might be tempted to conclude that I have remarkable powers quite beyond the grasp of other people. Finally, regarding *b*, we must be clear that correlation is not causation. What I mean is this: of course religious experience is associated with certain brain functions. So is eating. When I experience God, certain parts of my brain are active; when I experience eating, the same is true. But food is not an illusion.

That leaves us with options *a*, *d*, and *e*. It seems to me that *d* will satisfy no one. If God is real, why resort to *d*? If you do not believe God is real, you probably will not accept *d* either. Regarding *e*, the problem is that the environmental factors in which I experience God are the same as those for the vast majority of my other experiences, so to suggest that there *must be* some other factor that is not God, of which I am unaware, has so little evidence to support it that it is only an option if you have already decided that *a* must be impossible.

Which leaves option *a*. I seem to experience God, and these experiences occur repeatedly over time in normal circumstances. My experiences are usually a good guide to reality, and there are no compelling reasons to consider these experiences different in this regard. Therefore, I am a Christian because the most reasonable explanation of my experience of God is that I *am* in fact experiencing God.

19

BECAUSE OTHERS I KNOW HAVE EXPERIENCED GOD

I n the last chapter, I argued that the most reasonable explanation of my own experience of God is that I am truly experiencing God. However, if I were the only person claiming to experience God, we might quite properly question my claims. Why would I alone have such experiences? It would be natural to suspect that I was an anomaly, abnormal in some way, or a liar. Therefore, it is important to discuss the experience of others as an additional reason for considering the Christian faith to be the most reasonable faith to hold.

Trusting others

In general, each of us will tend to place different amounts of trust in what people say to us, depending upon our relationship with them and our prior experience. When a builder whom I have never met tells me he will pop over on Saturday to give me a quote, I will naturally trust this promise less than if he had worked for me before and had always been reliable and punctual. I will also consider someone reliable if that person's claims prove true over time: if my builder tells me the work will take two weeks, I will become convinced he is right when he packs his tools away after fourteen days.

Similarly, we will consider the information someone gives us more reliable if that person has come good in the past. If my friend tells me what time the bus is due, I am more likely to think him correct if he was right on a previous occasion. However, if I had missed the bus because he got it wrong, I probably would not ask him next time!

Finally, we also tend to trust what people tell us when it lines up with the way they live. For example, I am more likely to listen to someone tell me how to eat healthily if that person is not obese; I am unlikely to trust advice on giving up smoking when it comes from someone with a cigarette in the mouth. So, when people tell us something, it is more reasonable to believe them if:

1. We know them to be trustworthy.

2. They have been right on previous occasions.

3. Their words are not contradicted by their actions.

4. Their claims are confirmed over time.

Trusting others who claim to have experienced God

It is of course possible that you know someone entirely unreliable who claims to have experienced God, and you would be quite reasonable in rejecting that testimony as a good basis for Christian faith. However, it may well be the case for you, as it is for me, that the people you know who claim to experience God score quite well on all four of these criteria. They are generally trustworthy in life—usually, when they report an experience, it is reliable—they are not accustomed to delusion or lying.

Furthermore, some of these people may well have been right about numerous other aspects of life, from how to file a tax return to knowing a good place to go on holiday. They may generally be quite wise, intelligent, and helpful. If so, we may have rationally secure reasons to trust their testimony about their experience of God.

These reasons may be even better if we can observe that their experience of God correlates with the way they choose to live. If they claim to regularly experience a loving God but are relentlessly cruel, we have rational grounds for questioning their claims; but if they instead seem, over time, to be becoming increasingly loving people, their claims are more plausible. In fact, we may even know people whose lives appear quite dramatically affected by their claimed experiences; many people's claims to have experienced God are accompanied by a conversion in the way they live. They stop one way of life and increasingly choose a different way of life. Even when this is not dramatic, it may be possible to observe such people changing over time.

In fact, if we have the opportunity to get to know several people who claim to have experienced God, we may find ourselves able to see commonalities in their experiences and the consequent effect on their lives. We should expect significant differences as well, and, of course, we should also expect the occasional person to claim such experiences who does not fulfil our criteria for being trustworthy. Over time though, the more people we know, we are usually able to observe common threads.

If this is the case for us, that is, if we do know people who fulfil our criteria who claim to have experienced God, what is the most reasonable belief to hold? It seems to me that we must either conclude that although such people are generally reliable and trustworthy, we must think of them differently when they make claims to experience God; or we may consider their testimony as reasonable evidence that there is a cause of their experience that is true. If we choose the first option and reject their testimony on this issue, are we not being irrational? Why do we consider it logically consistent to accept their testimony on most issues in life but make an exception in this case? We must be honest about why we would consider that logical.

If, however, we are consistent and trust their testimony to some degree, we must then ask the same questions that I asked of myself in the last chapter. If they are truly experiencing something, what possible explanations are there? I think we would come up with the same list of possibilities and evaluate them in the same way as we did in the last chapter. It seems to me, then, that the most reasonable explanation is that in such cases, they are truly experiencing God; none of the alternative options is very plausible when it is really thought through to its logical conclusions.

In summary, I am a Christian not only because this is the best explanation of my own experiences, but it is also the most reasonable explanation of the experiences of other people whom I know to be generally trustworthy and reliable, especially when their claimed experiences accord well with the way that they live.

20

BECAUSE OTHERS I DON'T KNOW HAVE EXPERIENCED GOD

In the previous two chapters, we examined how the experience of God in our own lives and in the lives of those we know may serve as good evidence that Christian faith is reasonable. However, it may be possible to suggest that I and my acquaintances are merely one social phenomenon particularly influenced by the conditions of our time, location, and society. Perhaps our circle is somewhat unusual or an echo chamber distorting our view of reality? This is not entirely flippant, for we all know of the existence of cults or flat-earthers, or the certainty with which conspiracy theorists (and their followers) can believe something quite implausible. It is also important, then, to consider the experience of God reported by people whom I do not know personally and who come from a variety of sociocultural backgrounds.

Experience of God through history and culture

On this score, we must note three easily verifiable phenomena: 1) Christians who claim to experience God come from all over the world, from the full variety of social, national, racial, economic, and religious contexts. 2) This diversity is not only geographical but historical; the experience of God is claimed by Christians through all centuries of the last two millennia. 3) Although these experiences are hugely diverse, there is a remarkable continuity in what Christians mean by experiencing God, in the vast majority of cases—they describe similar experiences, interpreted in similar ways, with similar outcomes. Of course, it is not only Christians who report experiencing God, but to restrict our discussion to a manageable size, we will think only about Christian testimony at this point.

To elaborate on the first point: Christianity first emerged in the Greco-Roman world in the first few centuries CE but has since spread all over the world. We know of Christianity spreading in the capitalist West and Communist China, the repressive regime of North Korea, Islamic countries through the Middle East and Africa, the poorer global South and the wealthy global North. Of course, census data do not really give us much to work with regarding the experience of these people, but with the growth of the internet, it is increasingly easy to find books, videos, church services, individual stories, etc., from diverse groups that inform us about their experience of God.

To elaborate on the second point: the experience of God by Christians is not some recent phenomenon but is demonstrably present throughout the entire history of Christianity. From the first Christians onwards (including those who wrote the New Testament), we constantly read about the importance of the experience of God as a part of their lives and a reason for their faith. You can find this not only from the writings of "spiritual people" or clergy but in the lives of very ordinary people throughout the centuries.

To elaborate on the third point: reported experience of God from all of these groups tends to share some common emphases. Of course, there is diversity. Some report miraculous interventions of God in practical aspects of life; others focus on inner experience in the midst of suffering and oppression. However, if you take time to survey the evidence, it is remarkable how often the same sorts of themes emerge—the centrality of the person of Jesus; the giving and receiving of forgiveness; the experience of peace and hope; the power to love others, including those who are anti-Christian.

I am not claiming that all claimed experiences of God by Christians are reliable. The question is not "Are claims to experience God always true?" for the answer is always no. Neither is the question "Are all Christians throughout history reliable witnesses?" for that is also clearly not the case. The real question is, given the vast numbers of those who claim to experience God throughout history and our world, "What is the most reasonable explanation of that phenomenon?"

Possible explanations

It may help to list again the possible explanations for these experiences:

a. God

b. Individuals themselves

c. Other people

d. Other non-human spiritual beings

e. Other environmental factors

Let's take them in turn. If option *b* were true, then we would have to conclude that all of these people have individually generated experiences that they have then mistakenly attributed to God. It seems to me that this is hugely implausible: are people capable of deluding themselves repeatedly and in such large numbers, over such a long period of time, in such a variety of cultures, even if they do so unintentionally? Of course, some individuals may well be misinterpreting their experience, but to conclude that this is true of all Christians who have claimed to experience God seems a remarkably brave hypothesis.

We may approach option *c* similarly. It is of course true that many people first claim to experience God when interacting with other Christians, either in prayer, conversation, church services, etc., but the sheer numbers through space and time demonstrate that this is not a sufficient explanation. To take just one example, if the experience of God of the Christians in North Korea were caused only by the influence of others, we may have difficulty explaining why those Christians continue to experience God when Christianity is made illegal and is oppressed and gatherings of Christians are banned.

As we have previously discussed, option *d* satisfies no one, so we are left with option *e* as our only alternative; but this is perhaps the most implausible of all, given our discussion. We have already seen that Christians claiming to experience God emerge from all kinds of different environments. The chances of finding a couple of environmental factors that sufficiently explain their common experience in such diversity seems to me to be an impossible task. So we are left with option *a*.

In summary, there are some people who claim to experience God but whom we might rationally consider unreliable and therefore reasonably dismiss their stories as good evidence for the plausibility of their faith. However, I am a Christian because when we survey the sheer number and variety of claims, throughout history and across the globe, the most reasonable explanation is that there is in fact a God who stands behind, and is the ultimate cause of, these experiences.

SECTION 3.2

EXAMINING EXPERIENCE

Change

21

Because It Works

In the introduction, I suggested that a reasonable worldview is one that we can live out in practice—where our actions line up with our beliefs; as we have gone on, I have pointed out several places where I think we can see conflict between some worldviews and our common human behavior. It follows, then, that one of the ways we might test a worldview is by trying to live it out. Jesus made a claim along these lines when he said this: "If you do what I say, you are truly my followers, and you will know the truth, and the truth will set you free."[1] In other words, if we want to know whether or not what Jesus teaches is true, one of the ways we can find out is by following his teachings. Jesus claimed that as we do so, we will come to know, by our own experience, that his worldview is true (that it corresponds with reality) and that living in accordance with his way will set us free (that we will live the lives we are made to live). I am a Christian because I have become convinced that Jesus is right. To put it far too crudely: following Jesus *works*.

---

1. This claim is recorded in the Bible in the book called John, chapter 8, verse 31.

The way of freedom

It may help to give three very brief examples. First, one of the big themes in Jesus's teaching is that we are to forgive those who hurt us. By this he meant recognizing the wrong behavior and facing the pain it has caused but then releasing the other person from the need to somehow pay for what that person has done to us. He emphasized that each of us constantly needs forgiveness for our own wrongdoing and that God is the kind of God who is willing to forgive us. We, therefore, are to offer the forgiveness to one another that we each need from God. Jesus taught his followers to pray every day for forgiveness, both to give and receive it. When we put this into practice, we discover the truth: the fact is that we each hurt others, and are hurt by them, on a regular basis. Of all the possible responses (pretending it has not happened, revenge, resentment, excusing wrong behavior, ostracizing others, isolating ourselves, etc.), forgiveness regularly proves to be the best response—the one that sets us free.

Second, in the culture of the time, one moral maxim was "Do good to your friends and harm to your enemies." This was simply commonsense morality for the ancients; but Jesus commanded his followers to love their enemies—not in the sense of being a passive doormat for everyone to walk over, or of failing to resist evil when it is our responsibility to do so (after all, Jesus was killed for his words and actions), but instead, rather than repaying evil with evil, responding to wickedness with kindness. Like forgiveness, when people *do* this, they often find it to be the most life-giving response to injustice or suffering caused by others. This is true even if their actions do not change the attitude or behavior of the other person.

Finally, when confronted with human anxiety for the material necessities of life, Jesus advised that we should trust God to provide for us and show this in our actions by giving our money to the poor. To be generous when we feel financially vulnerable is not the kind of advice you will receive at your local bank; but again, those who have learned to live like this regularly say that it is a far more powerful antidote to anxiety than any other response. It can also be one of the ways we begin to know God, but that is beside the present point.

A difficult way

I hope I am not making it sound like doing what Jesus says is easy. Some of Jesus's commands are easy enough to understand (giving money to the poor is not a difficult concept in theory), and others are more complex. The point, though, is that *understanding* his teaching is not the primary challenge; doing what Jesus says is difficult mainly because it does not come naturally to us to *put his teaching into practice*. It can be hard to forgive someone who has betrayed us, or to love a noisy neighbor, or to sacrifice our own desires for the good of someone else. Nor does any of this tend to happen quickly. All meaningful human behavior is learned gradually, and this is no different. To do what Jesus says takes practice over time.

I should also clarify that we are not expected to do this on our own by sheer willpower. Jesus said that as we try to do what he teaches, we will be helped by God and, therefore, that learning to connect to God (through prayer, for example) is an important part of how we follow him. In fact, learning to experience God's power helping us to do what Jesus teaches is exactly the kind of thing that Jesus is talking about when he says that "you will know the truth."

Unavoidably personal

Doing what Jesus says is not an easy or quick experiment, but if we are willing to take the plunge, it is one of the ways we can test the Christian worldview. Of course, this chapter is a bit different from many others in the book in that it is an argument that you can only really evaluate in practice. There is no objective or detached way to decide whether what I have said has any merit to it; rather, it would require an unavoidably personal experiment. You are probably unlikely to do this unless other reasons have made you think that Christianity may be worth exploring, which is fine. As ever, if this chapter is not helpful, feel free to move on to one which is more resonant. It must be said, though, that all of us are always living out one worldview or another, so we are never truly detached from personal involvement. For some of you, it may be that your current worldview so clearly does not work (or has become self-contradictory or untenable in some other way) that to take the plunge as I have suggested really is the best way for you to continue your journey of discovering a reasonable faith.

I am a Christian because I have observed both for myself and for others that as we actually do what Jesus said, we not only learn that this worldview is true from the inside, but we become liberated to be people who are ever more fully alive.

22

BECAUSE INDIVIDUALS
ARE CHANGED

If the last chapter holds true (that is, if as we follow Jesus we come to know the truth and this truth sets us free to live fully human lives), then we should expect Christians to be people who are changing. Of course, all of us are constantly changing in certain ways—for example, the changes that come with aging or the way we are influenced by our culture—but in this chapter we are talking about change in *who we are* as people. Wrinkles are inevitable, but they may be the wrinkles of repeated smiles or of repeated frowns. My contention is that most people who become Christians do indeed begin to change on the inside: in their identity, character, and approach to life.

Changed lives

From the earliest days of the church, there have been dramatic conversions. Perhaps the most well known is that of a man called Paul, who was busy persecuting the first Christians when he had an experience of Jesus that transformed his worldview and caused him to spend the rest of his life starting new churches. I could cite many other examples from history but also an abundance from our own time. Every year will see the publication of another raft of books by people whose lives have been dramatically turned around by their experience of Jesus—and there will be even more on the internet. From addiction, atheism, despair, New Age, corporate success, hedonism, other religions . . . such stories are not hard to find if you want to hear them. Of course, we rarely know such people personally and that might leave us skeptical, a reaction with which I am sympathetic; for, after all, most of us have encountered tales of people whose claims are fantastical or insane. However, even if we were to doubt 90 percent of the stories we hear, there would still remain an enormous weight of testimony that cannot be entirely dismissed with a skeptical wave of the hand. Despite the lunatic fringe, there are so many stories of dramatic change that we need some kind of explanation that is not simplistic denial.

Having said this, to emphasize stories of dramatic change would be irresponsible. For most Christians, change is real but gradual. I work as a pastor, accompanying the people in my church on their journey with Jesus; gradual change is the norm, and dramatic change is the exception. As an example, we might think of the command of Jesus to give away our money as a response to worrying about how much money we have. Few are those who immediately give half their salary to the poor! Often, it begins by giving *something*, no matter how small, then perhaps a little more. As you experience that, despite having less, God provides for your needs, you are able to give away a significant amount, say the 10 percent that many Christians give. Over time, this becomes a habit. Having become familiar with this giving/God-providing dynamic, we become naturally more generous, not only with our money but with our possessions, time, and energy. Those who know Jesus well may even give away more than they can afford, choosing to live in an economy of grace. So much important change is like this. It is *not* inevitable; it is change we experience only when we are deliberately making choices to live a certain way. It is change in which we have responsibility, but we are also empowered by God to keep going. It is change that often comes gently, but these small adjustments over time add up to transformed people.

I know such change occurs because I have seen it repeatedly. Of course, if you do not know many Christians well, you may not have been able to observe such changes and remain skeptical. The other possibility is that you *have* known Christians and it has not been a pleasant experience . . .

What about bad or static Christians?

If you have known Christians who have treated you badly or, to return to our example of money, have been tight, you may think I am stupidly idealistic or naïve. I may seem to be painting a picture of wonderful people becoming even more wonderful, whereas the Christians you know are distinctly ordinary or perhaps even unpleasant. Well, I know a few of those as well (I fear, sometimes, I may even be one of them). If I want to make the claim that Christianity changes people to be more like Jesus, then I need to offer some explanation of those who do not seem to change.

The first thing to say is that it is entirely possible to call oneself a Christian, or even to think of oneself as a Christian, without following Jesus. Just like every other worldview or label, it can be misappropriated. Jesus once said that we would know who really followed him because they would be doing what he commanded. So, we might want to distinguish between the label and the life; it is those who are living the way of Jesus who are going to change.

Second, even those who really follow Jesus are not going to be perfect people. In fact, the whole point of change is that we are far from perfect! The Christian worldview is quite clear that we are all sinful, which means both that we do wrong things and also that we are not as we should be—we are broken or sick, in various ways. When we come to follow Jesus, we are forgiven and the process of healing begins, but (once again) it takes time. Sometimes Christians behave badly, and this is to be expected.

Third, we might add that we all start the journey from different places. Some of us have been raised in secure, loving homes, where kindness comes more easily because we have known much of it in life; others have suffered greatly and will take much longer to learn to love well. In this, we must also again remember the kind of God Christians claim exists. He does not override our choices to polish us up; he gently invites us to change without forcing us to move more quickly than we can.

Change observed

It is always possible to pick a single example, either good or bad, on which to rest your argument. This is not a very good approach to discovering the truth, for there are always exceptions and human oddities. Instead, we must try to get some sense of the overall picture, paying more attention to those who are trying to live out their worldview in practice. My hope is that if you know someone who has chosen to follow Jesus, you will not find that person faultless, but you will notice a change. You may find, as C. S. Lewis suggested, that the person may love you more but need you less. John Newton put it like this: "I am not what I might be, I am not what I ought to be, I am not what I wish to be, I am not what I hope to be; but thank God I am not what I once was . . . by the grace of God I am what I am."[1] I am a Christian partly because of the real change that I see in the lives of individuals as they follow the way of Jesus, which not only gives me confidence that this worldview is true but that it is good.

---

1. John Newton, as cited in *The Westminster Collection of Christian Quotations*, compiled by Martin H. Manser (Louisville: Westminster John Knox Press, 2001), 153.

23

BECAUSE SOCIETIES
ARE CHANGED

In the early years of the church, Christians were a tiny minority in the Roman Empire. Their writings indicate that these small communities attempted to shape their lives around the way of Jesus and in doing so experienced the kind of change we discussed in the last chapter. The change of individuals was intimately tied to the community of the church that always understood itself to be pursuing a way of life in contrast with the society in which it existed, in certain important ways. At first, then, these alternative communities were centers of change but only for those within them. However, as Christianity flourished, it had an increasing influence on society, and after the fourth-century Emperor Constantine (when Christianity became the religion of the empire), Christianity proceeded not only to change individuals but the entire culture. Once again, such change was not quick, but it was transformational.

Worldview

The transformation of society by Christianity is inseparable from the Christian worldview. It was where these beliefs and values contrasted with those of the Greco-Roman world that we see the origins of change. I will touch on four important points, most of which have already come up in other chapters.

Worldview

The value of life

One of the most important developments in the early church was the recognition that the death of Jesus was not only for the sake of the Jewish people but for the rest of the world as well. Forgiveness, life, and the way of Jesus were offered to all. This realization allowed Christians to understand the biblical idea of people being created in the image of God as applying to all and laid the foundations for an ethic that understood every human life to have intrinsic value (even slaves, foreigners, and women, in contrast to dominant Greco-Roman ethics).

Charity

Jesus modeled and taught that we should love not just those who love us (the ethics of his time) but should love those who cannot repay us, who do not deserve our love, and even our enemies. This other-directed love is summed up by the older meaning of charity (which may be expressed by giving our money to the poor but refers to more than this). The call to love was focussed on the obedience of the giver (to love like God loves) rather than the worthiness of the receiver.

Power and weakness

The cross was a brutal and shameful method of execution, usually reserved for slaves and particularly offensive criminals. Jesus's crucifixion marked the rejection of his message and his apparent failure. Obviously, the resurrection put things in a new light, but it is notable that it was the cross that became the symbol of the Christian faith. The life-through-death model of Jesus taught a power-through-weakness worldview. Many times, in the earliest Christian writings, the authors discuss the need to embrace weakness, suffering, powerlessness, and rejection and expected that, paradoxically, it was in these situations that the power of God would make the difference. Thus, Christianity placed a huge critique of human power at the heart of its worldview. The church did not always resist the temptation to power and was repeatedly guilty of misusing it, but nonetheless a subversive critique of power was so deeply embedded that it became a source of reform time and again.

The goodness and order of the world

In Greco-Roman philosophy, the material world was accorded fairly low value. It was the realm of the senses, coarse physical desires, or degrading manual labor. Gnosticism was a highly influential movement in the early centuries of the Common Era that also devalued our physical materiality, teaching a way of salvation that required an escape from this world. It influenced some early Christians before being firmly rejected by the church as a whole. Instead, Christianity saw the world as fundamentally good—created to display the glory of God. The material-physical life of humans was also good, and salvation was not an escape from this world but the redemption of it. As such, the Christian worldview took a positive view of nature (ordered rather than chaotic, to be enjoyed rather than rejected).

Consequence

To see each human as having intrinsic value, altruism as being a virtue, power as accountable, the natural world as ordered and good—my guess would be that those of us reading this book would think that these are obviously right ways of thinking. They seem

SECTION 3.2: EXAMINING EXPERIENCE

like common sense, but this is only because we have grown up in a culture that has been deeply shaped by Christianity over millennia; in pre-Christian times this was absolutely *not* how people thought. The transformation of worldview stands behind numerous practical changes in society as the centuries passed. We have already discussed the rise of science, the investment in education, and the establishment of forms of poor-care. We might add the development and reform of justice systems and prisons, medical care, the abolition of slavery, the flourishing of various art forms, the development of democracy (and other structures to limit or balance power), and the human rights project.

Of course, not everything that has been done under the label of Christianity has been good (or consistent with the Christian worldview). One may think, for example, of periods of forced conversions or some of the horrors of colonialism. It is also true that the full implications of the Christian worldview were not always worked out in practice, or at least not quickly—for example, the endurance of racism and the fact that the abolition of slavery came so late. However, it is only by the standards Christianity itself has given us that we look back with judgment. Christian society has not always lived up to its own standards, but it has transformed the standards by which we evaluate society.

Familiarity and contempt

Some will want to argue that although Christianity may have been very important in the development of all kinds of positive parts of Western culture, we should now keep those benefits whilst dispensing with Christianity. I wonder whether this is possible in the long term (as the dominant worldviews will always shape society), but that debate is not the point of this chapter. Rather, I have attempted to show what sort of changes accompany a society that is largely shaped by the Christian worldview. Many of the ways we now think are indebted to this process but are so familiar to us that we do not realize that *it was not always like this*. The legacy of the Christianization of our culture is a gift to which we stand so close, we may miss it altogether. It is only when we take the time to stand back and examine our social history that we can begin to understand the transformative impact of Christianity on society—change that is deep and, overall, deeply good.

To conclude this chapter then, I am a Christian partly because Christianity has shown the ability to transform (and keep reforming) culture in ways that better enable human flourishing. The process is imperfect and always in need of further change, but this is exactly what the Christian worldview would lead us to expect. Thus, again, it appears to be not only true but good.

SECTION 3.3

EXAMINING
EXPERIENCE

Desire

24

THE BEAUTIFUL WAY

M ost chapters in this book take a view from the outside, in that they discuss why I find Christianity to be the most reasonable faith in making sense of phenomena we can all observe. However, it would be dishonest to make out that these are the only reasons why I am a Christian, for there is also the view from the inside—the dimensions of the Christian worldview that become more important to us the more we live into them. In this and the following two chapters, I want to try to articulate three dimensions of this view from the inside for two reasons. First, the subtitle of this book is *Why I Am a Christian*, and they are part of the honest answer to that question. Second, these chapters will flesh out something of what the experience of following Jesus and coming to know God is like, which might be helpful for understanding why Christians find their faith reasonable; it may help to show some of how the Christian worldview hangs together in practice.

The first dimension is this: I am a Christian not just because I consider the worldview of Jesus to be true but because I find it to be overwhelmingly beautiful.

Grace

For Christians, God created all that exists, not because he needed to but because he wanted to. Because God did not *need* anything (he is always the perfection of love, joy, and peace), then everything he created is a gift of love. He did not create us to meet some lack in himself but *chose* to create us and invite us to enjoy all that he gives. Essentially, that means that the foundation of reality is *grace*, by which I mean we are loved and gifted existence by nothing more than the desire and goodness of God. To live into this belief is to let go of all attempts to earn love or to justify our existence (to ourselves or others); it is to let go of transactional relationships that operate on a tit-for-tat basis. Instead, we are called to love in a way that is united with the love of God and becomes increasingly marked by grace.

Christians believe that God demonstrated this kind of love when he himself became a man in the person of Jesus, who loved, suffered, and died for the very people who killed him. Following his example, we learn to love others, not because they deserve it or because they are particularly lovely, but because we want to gift them our love unconditionally. We learn to receive such love from others, not needing to always pay it back in some way or to strive for self-sufficient independence. As our love for one another becomes given rather than earned, it also becomes more natural to forgive, for our love does not depend on one another performing well in the relationship. Our lives become surrendered into the love of God, and we learn to live in the ways of grace.

Justice

God ultimately underwrites justice. He has created a world in which humans need justice to flourish (as we explored in a previous chapter), and he will ensure that, in the long run, justice will always be done (see "Hope" below). When grace is the basis on which we live and love, then wrongdoing can be properly confronted. Grace does not minimize or ignore evil but allows us to face it (in ourselves and in others) without the fear that we will no longer be loved.

For the Christian, as we come to know God's love, we also come to know his justice and become more aware of our own failures. We find God *convicts* us of our need to change—where our selfishness, ego, pride, thoughtlessness, ingratitude, envy, lust, and all other kinds of inordinate desires are harming ourselves and others. Justice convicts us; grace gives us the safety to bring our mess to God and ask for help. We also bring our mess to one another in confession. When we let others see our failures, we affirm together the importance of justice, give and receive grace, and help one another to change. Finally, we are called to work for justice in the wider community and society. The desire for justice is not an illusion but a mark of being made in the image of God and a call to confront evil and pursue the good in every area of life.

Hope

Jesus, who embodied the grace-filled love and uncompromising justice of God, was killed. But he was then resurrected. We, too, will die, but we, too, will be resurrected. There is a life after this life, not where we will sit around on clouds in an eternal church service (who could endure that!) but where life is restored to all that it was meant to be. We are free to fully enjoy the pleasures of God in a world where injustice is finally removed and everything is put right. The Christian life is therefore one of profound hope. Apparent disasters do not lead to despair, because Jesus showed us that life often comes through death. We can enjoy the goodness of material pleasures, but we do not have to grasp at them, knowing that nothing truly good will be lost to us in the long run. We can live fully engaged lives, pouring ourselves out for the sake of our broken world, holding on to a vision and hope for the transformation of our society. We can even face suffering and death, because we know that this is not the end, and, in this sense, we have got nothing to lose. Finally, this is the kind of hope that allows us to keep going in the long term. Ultimately, God is the one who stands behind all reality and will ensure the final victory of love and justice, so we can be at peace with living the lives to which he calls us, even if we cannot see success; we can relax when our progress is imperfect.

A cause to live for

It is painful to give such brief descriptions of such complex and beautiful realities, but I hope it gives a flavor of what it is like to experience Christianity from the inside; this is the shape of the lives we learn to live. Obviously, to accept these truths and learn this way takes a lifetime, but as we do so, the feeling we have is something like "this is how life was meant to be." It is not the sense of having reached the destination but of having finally found the right path. Such experience not only makes us more confident in the truth of our faith but also nurtures an ever-growing desire for God who is the source of this way of life. So, I am a Christian partly because of how compellingly beautiful it is from the inside to live into the grace, justice, and hope of God, a life that feels both true and meaningful, where the foundation of reality is also the fulfilment of desire.

25

The Need to Trust

The word *faith* can be used in many ways. In the introduction, I defined faith as "opinions we hold about anything that cannot be proved absolutely" to try to make clear that there is no conflict between faith and reason. In this chapter, though, I would like to explore another (related) use of faith, which holds true both in modern English and in the older languages—the use of faith to mean something like trust. We might talk of keeping faith with someone when we maintain our trust in that person, or we might say a faithful lover is one we can trust to remain true. It seems to me that the difference in resonance between belief and trust is that the latter seems more appropriate when talking of people. We believe that the earth is round, but we trust that our friend will keep his word; we believe that an airplane can fly, but we trust the pilot to fly us safely. The distinction is perhaps fairly minor; the key point for our discussion is that to talk of faith is often also to talk of the need to trust.

The human need to trust

I argued at the very start of this book that we all have a faith, in that we all believe things we cannot prove beyond all possible doubt.

In this sense, we are always already trusting in what cannot be fully known. Most of the time, this trust is a trust in others. We must trust the knowledge passed on to us by other humans and the conventions in which we live in order to do anything at all. For example, when I receive a bundle of bank notes in exchange for my labor, I do so trusting that these thin sheets of polymer (in themselves fairly worthless) will be considered valuable to those whom I hope will sell me some food. I put that money in a bank because I trust that the bank will keep it safe. When you really think about it, so many of our actions express the need to trust, a need that becomes even more evident when we take account of how little control we really have of our lives. Our health, employment, an ordered society, security of our possessions and even of our own lives—all of these can be taken away overnight, and regularly have been. The pressing problem with these bigger parts of our lives is that, for many, it is far from clear who or what could be *trusted* to offer us any kind of security.

When we cannot trust

If our relative lack of power and firsthand knowledge requires us to trust, then it is perhaps no surprise that those who struggle to trust face severe difficulties. It seems to me that if we cannot trust, we tend to respond to the insecurities of life in broadly two ways. First, we can strive for maximum control. This could look like the cynic who tends to suspect any information given by others as an attempt at manipulation, refusing to be taken in at any point; or, alternatively, it may be an obsession with our diet, avoiding eating anything that may make us more susceptible to various health conditions. Sadly, it is often the case that the further we pursue control of our lives, the more dehumanized our behavior becomes.

The second alternative to trust is to be consumed by the ravages of anxiety. We may give up on the possibility of control but be constantly haunted by the worries of an uncertain present and an unknown future. Again, the further down this road we travel, the more we seem to exchange living for merely surviving. Tragically, sometimes these two responses come together and become mutually reinforcing. I do not blame anyone who suffers in such ways; those actions may be the most logical response to materialist worldviews that ultimately tell us that we are dispensable organisms in a brutal universe. Of course, there are others who have the same worldview but live with a confident trust in . . . well, what exactly? We might wonder if such people are truly living in line with their worldview.

Trust in the Christian worldview

In the last chapter, we described how Christians are called to live surrendered lives in which we learn to entrust every part of our lives to the grace of God. There are two important reasons that we can do so: first, because God is the one in control, and second, because he is good; we can trust both his power and his love. To elaborate on the first point, if God is the source of all that is and who stands behind all reality, giving it its existence, form, beauty, and meaning, then he can be trusted in the sense that there is nothing to which he is subject and nothing that is beyond his control. However, power on its own cannot command trust, but only power combined with goodness. This goodness can be seen in many ways, but the most important is in the incarnation of Jesus: the God who holds all reality in his hands became embodied, taking human form and entering the mess, suffering, and struggle of a fully human life. It is not that we have somehow reached up for God but rather that he came down amongst us. We see his goodness in the life of Jesus, his love in the suffering of Jesus, his grace in the death of Jesus, and his power in the resurrection of Jesus. He asks us to trust him by following his way. We trust him because he has proved his love.

This life of following Jesus is therefore explicitly a life of trust (hence, faith). This is not a simplistic trust, where God acts as a divine insurance policy to guarantee a safe and happy life (quite the opposite, in fact). Rather, it is a trust in which we discover that whatever happens in life, we are *held*; a trust that enables us to see that evil and suffering can be transformed into gifts of love and glory; a trust that knows that all that is wrong now will one day be put right; a trust that can always hope, knowing that our hope will not be ultimately disappointed, because of who we are trusting. Like other aspects of the Christian life, this is not an easy or automatic way of living but one that we learn. We grow in our trust of God over time (much as we do with any person)—growing in the freedom of letting go of control, becoming quicker to give and slower to grasp, peace overcoming anxiety bit by bit.

The unavoidable choice

This is the second dimension of the view from the inside. We all have to trust, at least to some extent; it is the only way we can live, and to try to avoid this reality does us great harm. However, many worldviews give us no reason to be confident that such trust is meaningful. I am a Christian partly because I find that this worldview not only fits with the reality of our need to trust but demands it. If to be human is to trust, I find that it is the way of Jesus that makes me most human.

26

CALLED

This chapter is the final view from the inside, attempting to flesh out something of the experience of being a Christian. The third dimension I want to describe is the sense that I not only choose to follow, but am also called into the way of Jesus. Before I do so, it is worth repeating that there is no antithesis between experience (in this case, feeling called) and rational evaluation; we do not jettison the one in favor of the other. I have argued repeatedly that reasonable belief must account for both. So, by attempting to describe the experience of being called, I am not implying an emotional surge that overrides our rationality, but I do mean the sense that I am not the only agent, or person, that is involved in my journey.

Humans as whole people

Throughout history and across all cultures, humans have asked the big questions. We seem to have an insatiable desire for discovering what is true—the need to search for meaning and to make sense of life. It is often a discomfort with our current answers (that is, our current worldview) that makes us question and explore. Such discomfort can begin in different ways, given the various elements of what it is to be human. Sometimes, it can be intellectual: we come to see that our worldview is not as rationally coherent as we once thought, or that it is self-contradictory, or cannot explain the data of life. Other times, it is more emotional in its origin: we *feel* dissatisfied, having desires and longings that cannot be reconciled with our current understanding of the world. Alternatively, it may be that we have certain experiences that cannot be explained by our current worldview. When this is the case, we cannot simply go back to where we were before but must move forward . . .

The voice of God

What is first experienced as discomfort can come to be recognized not only as something about ourselves but something in which we hear the voice of another. It is the sense of being called on from where we are now to explore something different or, perhaps better put, to be invited deeper into truth. In the face of beauty, the pangs of desire call us to a beauty beyond what we currently know; in the barrenness of our days, we feel called to discover a life that is more meaningful and satisfying. It is not unusual to have a time in life where coincidences seem to mount up, where we feel nudged forward by an other who seems to be drawing us to themselves. In these or in other ways, we sense the move of our hearts towards something beyond.

The sense of being called is not only present at the start of the Christian life but comes again and again, in different ways and at different times. I have found that this can occur most power-fully not when I am eagerly seeking God but when I am closest to forgetting him or have drifted from the way of Jesus. Often at such times, in a book or a conversation, an experience, or a moment of quiet, I have again found myself being called back or called on; desire reawakens, and the heart stirs from its slumber.

Called

The hound of heaven

This experience reflects one important thing the Christian worldview claims about God, which is that he is not a God to whom we have somehow to attain, but rather, he is a God who comes to us. In contrast with some other worldviews, we do not achieve relationship with God through our moral behavior, meditative or religious success, rigorous self-discipline, magic spells or rituals, sufficient knowledge or understanding, or anything else that rests on our initiative. Rather, we are always responding to a God who takes the first move. He moves towards us, calling us, inviting us, alluring us. The ultimate demonstration of this is, again, in the coming of Jesus. God moved towards us by taking human form in order to reveal to us who he is, what he is like, and how we can live the lives for which we were created. Jesus described God as a shepherd who goes looking for his lost sheep; the poet Francis Watson described God as the hound of heaven who hunts down the objects of his love. In truth, although we often hear people talk about "finding God," the experience is most often more accurately like being found by God.

None of this should imply that we are passive in the process or that we are each to wait until we have some irresistible spiritual experience. That is not how it is either, for the Christian narrative also stresses the importance of our responsible choices and our ability to resist the invitation of God. This is again to do with the *goodness* of God: he will not use his power to manipulate us. His call will never be of such a kind that we cannot refuse (or refuse to acknowledge the existence of the call itself). There is always a choice.

Desire

This concludes the view from the inside. The aim of these chapters has been different from most of the others, in that I have attempted to describe more of what it is like to follow Jesus. It may help to show not only the inner coherence of the Christian worldview but why it becomes more reasonable as it is lived out in practice. It is as we come alive in the beauty of the way of Jesus, as we learn to trust the goodness and power of the God who is always calling us on, that we find ourselves knowing not only what seems to be true but the truth which sets us free.

Such belief is not and never can be detached. There is no conflict between being a Christian because we consider it to be the most reasonable and intellectually responsible worldview and being a Christian because we come to desire God and love the way of Jesus. We may start at one of these two points, but in the long run, they will lead to each other; for what is ultimately true is not the appropriate object just of our belief but also of our love.

SECTION 4.1

EXAMINING
THE OPTIONS

Why Christianity?

27

THEISM, PHILOSOPHY,
AND THEOLOGY

All the chapters of this book discuss the reasonableness of the
Christian worldview, but you will probably have noticed that
several of them present arguments that may also be made in de-
fence of other monotheistic worldviews. So why Christianity? This
is a fair question, and, although this is not a book in which to attempt any substantial comparison between different monotheistic
religions, these final three chapters will sketch the main reasons I
find Christianity to be the most compelling. Some of these we have
already touched on in previous chapters, but here I will make them
explicit and add a few others. In this chapter, we will tackle some
philosophical and theological reasons.

The Trinity

All monotheistic faiths claim that there is one God who is the foundation of all reality, who gifts all beings their existence and charges
life with meaning, purpose, and goodness. However, Christianity
is the only worldview that conceives of this God as Trinity, that
is, that this one God is manifest to us as three persons—God the
Father; God the Son, who is Jesus Christ; and God the Holy Spirit.

This one-essence-in-three-persons understanding of God was not a theological idea the Christians just came up with spontaneously, as it were, but rather it was the only way they could make sense of their experience of God—God who revealed himself in these three different persons. It would take a whole book to fully tease out the concept of the Trinity (and many such books are available); here we will concentrate on three ways this understanding of God makes a difference on a worldview level: why might God-as-Trinity be considered better able to make sense of life than other monotheistic conceptions of God?

Love

Although the great monotheistic faiths differ in their understanding of God, one similarity is that they all claim that God is the source and essence of love in one way or another—that our capacity to love is derived from God who embodies perfect love in himself. If that is the case, then God did not *become* loving at a certain point but has *been* love eternally, as he is the essence of love itself.

The tricky issue, though, is that love seems to require an object. What I mean is this: we cannot love in an abstract way; we need to love something or someone. There needs to be an other to love, or love is not love. The monotheistic religions claim that God pre-existed all that he created, so there was a moment where there was only God (or, to put it another way, there was the source of all being but no actual beings to which his love could be extended). This gives us a problem. How can God be eternally love when there is no one other than himself to love? And if he only became love when he created others, how can we say that love is part of God's essence?

The Christian worldview can here offer its understanding of God as Trinity—that the one God has eternally been three, united in one essence but distinguishable as persons. Thus, the Christian God has always been in a community of love, because love has always had an object. The Father loves the Son and the Spirit, the Son loves the Father and the Spirit, and the Spirit loves the Son and the Father. When the Bible claims that "God is love,"[1] it can do so because of the Trinity. There has always been an object for God's love, and so he truly *is* love in his essence.

Particulars (and universals)

If life has any meaning, it must be meaningful in two ways. First, there must be *universals*, categories of things or objective values that allow us to know anything. For example, imagine if every time we wanted to talk about an insect, we had to describe the various sizes, shapes, colors, and features of this thing to talk about it. That is not what we do. Instead, we have a category (insect, creature, etc.) that allows us to grow in knowledge; but if it is to be real knowledge, it must cover all the individual things—hence, it must be universal. This is most easily seen in science. We cannot talk about scientific *knowledge* unless this knowledge proves to be true for all of us (someone claiming to be able to build an ice palace in the Sahara clearly does not *know* a few things . . .). So, too, if concepts like love, goodness, evil, mercy, or truth are to have any objective meaning, they must be universal.

However, we must also find meaning for *particulars*. If there are only universal laws, then any particular thing becomes value-less. We have noted this as a problem for naturalism in previous chapters: if our existence is merely a set of physical laws mechanically playing out, what individual thing or person can be said to have any meaning in itself?

It seems, then, that for existence to have meaning, the source of all that exists must account for unity (and therefore universals) and also diversity (and therefore particulars). Other monotheistic faiths can account for unity but not diversity; polytheism can account for diversity but not unity. Here again, we see that the Christian understanding of God as Trinity, unified as one God yet diverse as three persons, is an understanding that is able to offer a

1. As it does, for example, in the book of First John, chapter 4, verses 7–12.

135

better philosophical answer for why both universals and particulars are meaningful.

Identity in Unity

Finally, to tease out one further implication of the last section, our world is full of examples of individual units coming together to create a unified whole, whether that is chemical compounds (made up of elements bound together), societies (individual people forming groups), marriages (two people uniting as one family), or organisms (cells working together). At every level of life, we can see this pattern. So, too, Christianity claims that those who follow Jesus will be progressively *united* with him but without losing their *identities* as people; again, the Christian worldview meshes with life as we all experience it. The ultimate rationale for this phenomenon must be sought at the source of all beings (why is our existence this kind of existence?), and, again, I would suggest that the Trinity is the concept of God that can offer the best explanation: existence constantly manifests identity in unity because it reflects the nature of God himself who is three-in-one.

Philosophical integrity

I am aware that many who read this will not enjoy philosophy and may find it difficult to get anything out of this chapter. That is fine; I hope the following pages will be of more use to you. But it is important at least to sketch these ideas because monotheistic religions do differ considerably in the claims they make about God, humanity, and existence, which means that we are rationally invited to distinguish between them as to which is more reasonable on philosophical grounds. As we do so, I find the Christian concept of God to be more philosophically and theologically robust, and therefore more likely to be true, which is one of the reasons I am a Christian.

28

NOTHING TO HIDE

There is a proverb, "Truth defends itself." Obviously, this is not always the case (ask anyone who has had a brush with the legal system), but it gets at something important, which is that if something is true, then it will, in the end, be able to stand up to the most thorough examination and critique. This is also the case with worldviews. We all tend to prefer the evidence that confirms what we already think and to read the books with which we agree, because it is uncomfortable to begin to question our worldview. However, if we are to be truly rational and personally honest, and if we want to know the truth, we must be prepared to subject our worldview (and others) to robust investigation. After all, we tend not to believe people who refuse to let their statements be properly tested—like the friend who boasts of having an impressive job but will not tell us where he or she works, or the scientist who claims to have made a research breakthrough but fails to publish the data. It is those who have nothing to hide who are likely to be telling the truth. I believe the same is true of monotheistic worldviews. If we want to distinguish between them, we may want to ask probing questions of them all. When we do so, I find I am a Christian partly because Christianity has nothing to hide.

Intellectually

In a sense, most of this book has addressed the intellectual integrity of Christianity, but it is worth making two points explicit here. First, throughout the last two millennia, Christianity has been exposed to the free consideration and critique of our finest minds. Many of those have themselves been or become Christians, but others have not, so Christianity has been thoroughly probed from both the inside and the outside. Although not all have been persuaded of its truth, it is clear that Christianity has been able to handle that process. More than that, it has come out stronger; tested by generation after generation, it has proved to be a remarkably robust worldview. Second, Christianity has also been shaped by the intellectual discoveries of each generation, without changing its fundamental claims. It has been able to embrace its Jewish heritage; the Greek tradition; and medieval, modern, and postmodern insights, integrating what is true in each of these and offering robust critique of what is not. In all this, it has not found itself, ultimately, in conflict with any other compelling truth claim. As such, Christianity welcomes any philosophical probing or intellectual inquiry. Any genuine truth-seeker will find the path well trodden.

Historically

Christianity claims that God has revealed himself in history through actual events and people. Certain things happened in history! As such, Christianity is open to historical investigation. Such investigation has its intrinsic limits, of course, as any good historian will be able to tell you, so it is not quite as simple as being able to prove or disprove all the historical claims of Christianity; but we can certainly examine how they stack up. When we do this, whether that is through archaeological research or comparing the Christian accounts of Jesus's life to other historical sources, we tend to find that they stack up well.

This becomes important because when Christianity claims that God has revealed himself to us, it is not primarily talking about an individual having a set of mystical experiences, which are then reported to be revelation from God, but rather that God has been revealed through the real man Jesus, his words and actions in history, which were witnessed and written about by many, and thus was from the very beginning open to critique and investigation.

Christianity has not been afraid of critical investigation of the Bible either—examining the texts' history, their sources, the way they were put together and edited, the formation of the canon (the process by which books came to be included in the Bible), other writings that were excluded, and all such questions that also fall broadly in the purview of history. Such is the bread and butter of many Christian scholars. Neither has it been ashamed of the history that comes before it: the historical claims of Judaism in which Christianity was birthed or the fact that many other religions existed before Christianity. There is no threat to the Christian worldview in such facts; it has no need to be afraid of history.

Culturally

Christianity became established in the Middle East, North Africa, and the Roman Empire but has since spread to most places in the world. It has grown and flourished in very diverse cultures. At times, this has been due to military conquest by powerful Christian rulers, but this is the exception, not the norm. For the most part, Christianity has not grown through conquest or violence but through sacrificial service and the communication of the message of Jesus. The Christian worldview is often considered Western, but this is primarily because the West has been so deeply shaped by Christianity; Christianity's Westernness is not intrinsically the case, as has been seen time and again in the non-Western Christian church.

Ethically

As we covered in a previous chapter, the moral standards that are now considered common sense were not always considered so. Their dominance now is largely due to the transformation of culture by Christianity that established Judeo-Christian morality as the norm. It is true that the church has, at times, behaved appallingly, but the very standards we use to make that judgment are rooted in the Judeo-Christian worldview. Two additional points may be made that distinguish Christianity from the other monotheistic religions. First, Christianity has become separable from any particular political system. It conceives of the church as an alternative community that is to serve the society in which it exists, not as a rival community that must ultimately demand political power (even though it may sometimes gain it). Second, this means that the Christian worldview not only expects others to think and live differently but compels Christians to defend their right to do so. It requires that people be treated as God treats them, recognized as individually valuable and possessing the responsibility of free will. This essentially hardwires tolerance into the center of the Christian social vision. Of course, there are times the church has not lived up to that (as can be said of all other worldviews), but Christianity by nature properly requires it.

Making the comparison

Christianity welcomes intellectual, historical, and ethical critique and an examination of how it has grown and developed over time. Moreover, there are important differences in each of these areas between Christianity and other monotheistic religions. Ultimately, I am unconvinced that any of the others have a tradition of intellectual/critical rigor or historical openness that can stand up to that of Christianity. Although many have grown, I question whether they have grown without conquest or whether they are able to transcend particular racial/ethnic cultures in the way that Christianity has. Finally, I remain doubtful that they have the built-in resources to be able to offer the same freedom of conscience and decision or the ethical tradition of Christianity.

The most important thing to say, though, is that you do not have to take my word for it. Examine the options, work through the evidence, search for the truth. I am a Christian because I find that when I do this, Christianity has nothing to hide.

29

BECAUSE OF JESUS

The previous two chapters sketched some of the reasons that I find Christianity more compelling than other monotheistic religions, but the most important of all is the person of Jesus Christ, the subject of this chapter.

The great divider

For those who are less familiar with Jesus, one of the things that can be surprising is just how offensive he was. He made it clear that he would bring division, and that proved to be the case: some died for him, and others killed him. The reason was not that Jesus proclaimed a challenging worldview (although he did) nor that he was a controversial religious reformist (although he was) but that he deliberately and systematically made it all about himself.

What I mean is this: Jesus regularly taught about God, about humanity, and about the way we should live, but in each of these areas, he made outrageous claims about himself. He claimed not only to have come from God and to know God but to *be* God—able to forgive sins and give eternal life. He claimed that no human could find life apart from through him—that he was the only way to God. He claimed that it was when we follow him and live his way that we become fully human and live the lives we were made for—that he is the light of the world. Ultimately, his claim to those who followed him was "If you have seen me, you have seen the Father [God]."[1] These statements make it hard to sit on the fence.

Over and over again in the accounts we have of Jesus's interaction with others, the primary issue he addresses is whether they are willing to follow him, to believe him, to trust him. When he drew together a community of people to travel and work with him, he said that *this* community—the one centered on him—was now more primary than his followers' own families. He placed loyalty to him at the center of the community and way of life he established.

It is these claims that are still the primary division between the great monotheistic religions. Jesus was a Jew who claimed to be the Jewish Messiah. Some Jews believed him and began the movement that has become Christianity; other Jews did not and took a different path (rabbinic Judaism, which became dominant and shaped Judaism as it is now). Islam accepts Jesus as a prophet but emphatically denies that he is God (the Qur'an makes this quite clear). Jesus is the great divider: he either is the Messiah (Christianity), or he is not (Judaism); he either is God himself become human (Christianity), or he is not (Islam).

Ultimately, if you are to accept or reject Christianity, it is the person of Jesus with whom you must finally wrestle. Many previous chapters have touched on the reasons I have followed him, but I will use the rest of this chapter to summarize why I find Jesus so compelling.

A king to follow

Jesus claimed to be the Messiah-King long awaited by the Jews, and he talked a lot about the kingdom of God, but when he was questioned by the Roman ruler Pilate, he was clear that his kingdom was not like other kingdoms . . .

---

1. In the account of John, chapter 14, verse 9.

Jesus was a king who came with power, in both his actions and his words. He was able to heal the sick (in mind or body); he was able to perform miracles (like multiplying food or stopping storms). He had lips of thunder, speaking truth to power, confronting hypocrisy, challenging and provoking those who heard him. His teaching turned lives around and his words were full of authority. He never compromised.

And yet this power was not applied in the way most kings use power. He never manipulated people; he never used his power to hurt or destroy, to threaten or intimidate. He repeatedly rebuked those who wanted him to be a military king and shunned violence. He was attentive to the poor, the weak, the sick, and the shamed but was also comfortable with the rich and privileged. He spent time with the honored and the despised. He respected people's choices. He invited, but he never compelled.

A shepherd to trust

Jesus was a king, but he spent a lot of time avoiding crowds. When he travelled and taught, he tended to skip the bigger cities, preferring the smaller ones. He spent his time with common people rather than seeking access to political and social elites. He seemed to have come for ordinary people.

He claimed to be the good shepherd who loves his sheep, and he walked that out in practice. He seemed to know just what was needed by each person he encountered. He had such compassion and grace: restoring a woman humiliated by her community when caught in adultery, spending his time with children when his followers thought children unimportant, offering forgiveness and his way of life to Jews hated by their community for collecting tax on behalf of the Romans. He knew when to confront and when to encourage, rebuke, or commend. Those who knew Jesus described him as the most righteous and blameless man who ever lived, and yet "sinners," those whose lives were far from blameless, flocked to him. They knew they were loved. He was the doctor who came for the sick, not the healthy.

A vision to live for

This shepherd-king claimed to be establishing a new kingdom, one of love and justice in which God's will would increasingly be done and human lives would be put right. Those who followed him lived and died for this vision. So do many today. This is, after all, the claim of Christianity: that Jesus was not just all these things in the past but that he is present and active now. He is a king we still follow and a shepherd we still trust. He is still at work changing the lives of normal people, calling them to live their lives in and for the kingdom of God. Obviously, this claim raises many questions that this book is not designed to address, but it is part of the true answer to "Why Christianity?"—because the shepherd-king Jesus, and his call into the kingdom of God, is utterly captivating.

The worldview and the way

This is the ultimate answer to the question of "Why Christianity?" The monotheistic faiths divide here, both on a worldview level and the way they call us to live. Even the name Christianity emphasizes that this is those who accept the claims of Jesus and choose to follow his way; other religions do not. My burden in this chapter has been to show that this difference is central to what distinguishes monotheistic religions, not only in theory but in practice, not only in mind but in heart. It is a matter of theology and philosophy but also a matter of coming to terms with a person. If you want to make a choice between monotheistic worldviews, you need to wrestle with the person of Jesus.

30

CONCLUSION

A life of meaning and a meaningful life

There is an unerring human desire to make sense of life, to search for meaning and purpose in our existence. I have found that it is Christianity that is able to give the most satisfying answers in this quest. C. S. Lewis used a helpful metaphor when he claimed that he believed in Christianity for the same reason he believed in the sun, not just because he could see it but because he could see everything else by it. I find Christianity compelling in its claims not only because they make sense in themselves but because they make sense of the life that we experience.

But, in truth, this is only half the story. It is not just that Jesus makes sense of life but that he shows us how to live. There is a worldview, but there is also a way. I am a Christian because I find it is as I follow Jesus that I live a meaningful life. As I learn his way, there is a continual growth in knowing the truth, intellectually and in practice. It is knowing a worldview and knowing a way, but finally, it is also knowing a person. And does not this itself speak to the deepest reality of being a human being—that at bottom it is a question of relationship—to love and be loved? After all, love is the most profound kind of knowledge.

Conclusion

An examined life without and within

This book has appealed to your mind. I have sought to explain why I find Christianity to be the most reasonable faith to hold. I hope, however, this does not give the impression that making sense of life can ever be a detached or purely intellectual process, for we are already living! There is no neutral viewpoint from which to objectively assess all the possibilities, for we all already have a worldview and have embarked on life.

For this reason, relatively few people will become Christians because of the rational case for Christianity alone, strong though I hold it to be. For all of us, we have already been shaped by our experiences and upbringing, and if we really want to find the truth, we may need also to investigate how that affects our perception of the world. Paul Vitz, for example, has argued convincingly that there is a strong link between firm atheism and those who have been deprived of a positive father figure.[1] All of us need to be aware of our predispositions and how that may hinder our exploration.

Another factor that gets in the way of an evenhanded examination of life is our willfulness. Often we have built our lives on one worldview and do not really *want* to consider the possibility we may be wrong. The American philosopher Mortimer Adler was honest enough to say in his autobiography that "the simple truth of the matter is that I did not wish to live up to being a genuinely religious person."[2]

For these reasons and more, coming to terms with the Christian worldview in a detached way, and understanding its coherence and plausibility in theory, may not be enough for you. You may need to taste and see . . .

1. Paul C. Vitz, *Faith of the Fatherless: The Psychology of Atheism*, 2nd ed. (San Francisco: Ignatius, 2013).

2. Mortimer Adler, *Philosopher at Large* (New York: Macmillan, 1977), 316.

Coming Alive

If you have read to the end of this book, you have begun to consider the Christian worldview, but at the center of that worldview is a way—the way of Jesus. Jesus said from the beginning that it is as we *do* what he says that we will know the truth and that this truth will set us free. It is no surprise, then, that most of those who convert to Christianity do so once they have known other Christians well enough to see what following Jesus is like in practice; it is as they get to know those who know Jesus that they consider getting to know him themselves. The worldview and the way—finding meaning in life and discovering a way to live meaningfully. Intellectually robust and emotionally engaging—the satisfaction of our inquiring minds and our desiring hearts. We might say, as Jesus put it, that this is coming to love God with your heart, mind and strength, which is also to become fully alive.

The risk

To explore Christianity in this way may feel like a risk. There may be the illusion of safety or detachment in an intellectual process (although it is only an illusion, for truth is always disruptive, however it is encountered), but to actually begin to get to know Christians and their community (a local church, perhaps), to start to read and do what Jesus says . . . these things require a different level of engagement. And to be honest, following Jesus will involve your life being turned upside down. Jesus was quite clear when he said, "If any want to become my followers, let them deny themselves, take up their cross and follow me, for those who want to save their life [i.e., to stay comfortable, secure and safe] will lose it, and those who lose their life for my sake will find it. For what will it profit them if they gain the whole world but forfeit their life? Or what will they give in return for their life?"[3] That's not exactly a trouble-free proposal. But then again, it was Jesus who made it,

---

3. You can find this in the account of Matthew, chapter 16, verses 24 to 26.

and ultimately, to follow him is to trust him. Of course, there is a risk, but the promise is that we discover life.

Christianity is a faith in the sense that it is a worldview, a set of beliefs that we cannot prove absolutely. I have tried to explain why I find it to be a faith that is more reasonable than any of the other worldviews on offer. But Christianity is also a faith in the sense of trust: it is about trusting the person of Jesus and following his way. And of course, just like with any person, you cannot be certain that he is trustworthy at the beginning. I guess there is only one way to find out.

Appendix

FURTHER READING

This book covers a lot of ground, but my discussion of each topic is quite brief. It may be that some readers want to investigate one or two of the arguments in greater depth and would appreciate some guidance as to where they might start. That is what I have tried to offer in this appendix by suggesting some further reading in relation to specific chapters or sections of the book. I have largely recommended books that are aimed at a popular audience, but I have also included one or two that are more demanding where it seemed necessary.

Chapter 1: Because There Is Something Rather Than Nothing

One of the best statements of this argument is still the first chapter of Francis Schaeffer's *He Is There and He Is Not Silent*, revised edition (Carol Stream, IL: Tyndale House, 2001). More demanding and wide ranging is the third chapter of David Bentley Hart's *The Experience of God* (New Haven, CT: Yale University Press, 2013).

APPENDIX

Chapter 2: Because of Science

Two short but helpful books that discuss the relationship between science and religion are John Polkinghorne's *Reason and Reality* (London: SPCK, 1991) and Alistair McGrath's *Surprised by Meaning* (Louisville, KY: Westminster John Knox Press, 2011). See too *It Keeps Me Seeking* (Oxford, UK: Oxford University Press, 2018) by Andrew Briggs, Hans Halvorson, and Andrew Steane. On the limitations of scientism/naturalism as a worldview, J. P. Moreland's *Scientism and Secularism* (Wheaton, IL: Crossway, 2018) is both instructive and concise. Finally, for those who continue to find the theory of evolution a barrier to Christian faith and want substantial help, Conor Cunningham's *Darwin's Pious Idea* (Grand Rapids: Eerdmans, 2010) is worth the work.

Chapter 3: Because Things Happen

This chapter discusses one of the classic arguments for the rationality of belief in God. As such, it has been stated and restated many times, but I find the fourth chapter of Dallas Willard's *Knowing Christ Today* (New York: HarperCollins, 2009) to be one of the most accessible and clear versions easily available.

Sections 1.2 and 1.3: Our Knowledge of Ourselves and Our Common Human Behavior

It is hard to offer suggestions for each chapter in these two sections, as few books tackle the topics individually. Instead, it may be more helpful to point to others who take a comparable approach with some overlap in content: Tim Keller's *Making Sense of God* (London: Hodder and Stoughton, 2016) is very accessible, as is the first part of Tom Wright's *Simply Christian* (London: SPCK, 2006). However, I still find C. S. Lewis to be the most compelling writer about these themes: his *Mere Christianity* (London: HarperCollins, 2012) is interesting, but his autobiography both in narrative form—*Surprised by Joy* (London: HarperCollins, 2012)—and in

metaphor—*The Pilgrim's Regress* (London: HarperCollins, 2018)—
are captivating. On language and communication (ch. 9), I must
acknowledge my debt to Rowan Williams's *The Edge of Words*
(London: Bloomsbury, 2014) and recommend his essays for a far
more complete account of this topic. Finally, the quotations of
Blaise Pascal embedded in the book demonstrate my dependence
upon his thinking, and for those who would like more, his *Pensées*
(London: Penguin, 1995) are cheap to obtain.

Section 2.1: The Resurrection

Lee Strobel's *The Case for Christ* (Grand Rapids: Zondervan, 1998)
is one of the most well-known popular discussions of the historical
evidence for the resurrection. Gary Habermas and Michael Licona
have written *The Case for the Resurrection of Jesus* (Grand Rapids:
Kregel, 2004), which is very methodical but with a somewhat grat-
ing style, clearly aimed at those who are already Christians. For
those who want something truly comprehensive, *The Resurrection
of the Son of God* (London: SPCK, 2003) by N. T. Wright is unsur-
passed. Chapter 18 will be the most pertinent, although it does not
stand apart from his argument as it progresses through the book.

Section 2.2: The Church

Again, it is difficult to recommend books that exactly parallel my
arguments in this section, but here are three more recent books
that may be of interest: first, Rodney Stark's *The Triumph of Christianity* (New York: HarperCollins, 2011); second, David Bentley
Hart's *Atheist Delusions* (New Haven, CT: Yale, 2009); third, Tom
Holland's *Dominion* (London: Abacus, 2020). Each in their own
way traces the history of Christianity and its influence into modern times.

Section 3: Examining Experience

This is perhaps the hardest section of all in which to make recommendations, due to both the quantity and variety of published material. After considerable internal wrestling, I have decided simply to recommend a couple of the books that I have found interesting; more are available. Aside from C. S. Lewis, who has already been cited above, my chosen books are: *The Autobiography of George Muller* (Springdale, PA: Whitaker House, 1984) and *The Heart of John Wesley's Journal*, edited by Percy Livingston Parker (Peabody, MA: Hendrickson, 2008). Regarding the argument from religious experience in general, you may wish to read chapter 13 of Richard Swinburne's *The Existence of God*, 2nd edition (Oxford, UK: Clarendon Press, 2004).

Section 4: Examining the Options

The best book I know for exploring the contrast between Christianity and alternative worldviews is James W. Sire's *The Universe Next Door*, 5th edition (Downers Grove, IL: IVP Academic, 2009), which is clear, robust, and very readable. For a fleshed-out account of the Christian worldview in relation to the Bible, see D. A. Carson's *The God Who Is There* (Grand Rapids: Baker Books, 2010). For a popular-level exploration of the trinity, Michael Reeves's *The Good God* (Milton Keynes, UK: Paternoster, 2012) may be helpful.

Printed in Great Britain
by Amazon